Show, Don't Tell

A Guide to Purpose Driven Speech

Second Edition

Jeri Warren

Show, Don't Tell
A Guide to Purpose Driven Speech

Edition 2

Copyright © 2015 by Jerianne Warren
Edited by Mark Warren
Cover Design by Rich Breyer

ISBN-13 9780615498355
ISBN-10 0615498353
BISAC: Language Arts & Disciplines / Public Speaking

Printed in the United States of America.

http://thespeakingguide.com

Contents

Introduction & Conclusion.. 1

   Exercise #1 The Nightmare 4

   Exercise #2 Spitting It Out... 15

Chapter One: Ready, Set, Yell 17

   Exercise #3 Concentration 19

   Exercise #4 The Introduction 24

   Exercise #5 The Difference....................................... 31

   Exercise #6 Watch Out, Shakespeare 35

Chapter Two: The Road to Showing, not Telling: 39

   Exercise #7 Improve with Improv 41

   Exercise #8 Quotations to Remember or Not.......... 44

   Exercise #9 The Demonstration 54

   Exercise #10 Index Card Almighty............................ 57

Chapter Three: Break a Leg.. 59

   Exercise #11 Pet Peeve 68

   Exercise #12 The Informative Speech....................... 78

   Exercise #13 Review the Index Card Almighty.......... 80

Chapter Four: It Isn't Just Words 81

   Exercise #14 Nuked Charades.................................. 82

   Exercise #15 Go Shopping.. 85

   Exercise #16 Pronunciation & Tone 95

Chapter Five: Ready, Set, Sell 101

   Exercise #17 *Macbeth*, Act 1, Scene 7 103

   Exercise #18 Making Your Audience Think Like You............... 106

Exercise #19 Movie Pitch, Elevator-Style.................................. 109

Exercise #20 Show Me à la M.M.S. 114

Exercise #21 The Commercial Copy 119

Chapter Six: Where's the Beef? 121

Exercise #22 The Sheets.. 130

Exercise #23 The Persuasive Speech Intro............................. 134

Exercise #24 Walk in Their Shoes... 135

Exercise #25 The Persuasive Speech...................................... 139

Chapter Seven: Weapons of Mass Discussion..................... 141

Exercise #26 Off the Cuff 147

Exercise #28 Rock the Boat.. 156

Chapter Eight: Red Bull for the Soul 157

Exercise #29 Improve Your Odds 159

Exercise #30 The Formal Introduction of That Special Person 165

Exercise #31 The Formal Introduction of You........................ 166

Exercise #32 The Road Not Taken.. 171

Exercise #33 The Road You Took 175

Appendix A: Irregular Verbs 177

Appendix B: Nuked Charades 183

Sources Consulted... 187

No matter what your dream is, the yellow brick road that leads you there is paved with effective verbal communication. If you learn to inform, persuade, entertain, motivate and inspire, you'll have to contend with fewer flying monkeys.

—Jeri Warren

Introduction & Conclusion

Never before have we relied so heavily on our media habits to dictate the way we communicate. Would you be able to power down for a weekend? Twenty-four hours? One hour?

In a world in which thumbs have replaced tongues, one in which texting has become an essential mode of communication, it's not unusual to enter a room where all eyes are on mobile devices and the only sound is that of fingers tapping away on them. It's easier and quicker to tweet, text or connect via Facebook than it is to make verbal contact. Unfortunately, the easier it becomes to communicate with fingers, the more difficult it can become to speak comfortably and effectively with our mouths.

That's a problem. Until the job interview, business meeting and classroom discussion evaporate, it is imperative that verbal communication remain alive and, well, verbal. But most of us shudder at the thought of public speaking whether or not we've grown up with a mobile device always in hand.

All "public" means is not alone. It doesn't matter if it's a conversation with a close friend or a stadium full of adoring fans—when you open your mouth to talk you're speaking publicly.

You may never run for public office or be a television personality, but there are plenty of times when you need to be captivating (when you want to charm someone), motivating (when you want to create change) and persuasive (when you want to convince your friends to go to the movie of your choice, not theirs).

For some of us, public speaking comes easily, but for most people it's tough to be an effective speaker.

As an actor and teacher, I still get nervous before stepping onto the stage or in front of a new class, but I have learned to use that fear to work for me instead of against me.

Show, Don't Tell lays out for you, in a clear, succinct manner, what it takes to not blurt expletives when you find out you have to speak in public. My book does not overload you with information but gets right to the point, with proven methods and lots of examples.

In this book, I do something I do in all my classes—emphasize the fun factor. When you are enjoying yourself, you are much more likely to step out of your comfort zone and try something new.

Of course, there are lots of good how-to books and DVDs on public speaking out there, but no one has ever learned how to speak effectively by just reading pages or watching video clips. And no book has ever told you in one sentence what it takes to be a great public speaker. That is, until now. Here's the sentence:

Always leave your audience wanting more.

If you can do that, close this book—you're done. This, for you, is the conclusion of *Show, Don't Tell*. If, however, you could use some pointers for always leaving your audience wanting more, read on.

Speech is an incredible tool that allows humans to convey ideas and facts. But throughout human history, telling through words alone has not been enough to do the whole job. In public speaking, your goal is to deliver more than just the words. You should deliver the feeling, the desire and the emotion that drives your purpose for giving a speech.

Show, Don't Tell: A Guide to Purpose Driven Speech shows you the steps needed to take your message beyond just telling and to always leave your audience wanting more.

This book is designed both for individuals, who can use it on their own or perhaps with a friend or two (what's a speech without an audience?), and for use in a classroom. The advice and exercises have proven to be successful for both types of readers.

My job as an instructor and as the author of *Show, Don't Tell* is to encourage you, help you develop your speaking voice, strengthen your knowledge of the tools and techniques for communicating with purpose, and steer you toward a real sense of confidence.

I affirm my students, but I do not lie to them when I give critiques. I strengthen them by sharing both my book knowledge and my experience. I lower my students' anxiety level by leading them in repeat performances.

This book mirrors my classes. In it, I let you know what it takes to give a strong speech, but it's your job to build your "muscles" by getting up and doing the exercises in this book.

I appreciate great orators and the steps we all take to emulate them. I warn you about the potholes of public speaking. I aim you in the right direction by keeping you focused on what you want to say, and I motivate you by making this book relevant and fun. I thank you and respect you for your commitment to improvement.

My hope is that you will respect the passion I have for the topic and tap into it. From my point of view, helping you become a better speaker is good. Helping you become someone whom people want to listen to is better.

Now, let's begin that relationship you are soon to have with an audience by becoming aware of your vocal cords and the sound that comes out of your mouth. The voice is not seen or touched, so for many it's still a stranger.

Exercise #1
The Nightmare

Turn off your mobile devices. Yes, power down. I understand this is a bit like telling some of you to stop breathing for the next ten minutes. Have no fear. It's just until the next exercise.

Now, remember four things: your name, where you were born, where you live currently and what you see yourself doing in five years.

Speak those four things—*out loud*.

Become aware of the sound of your voice.

Why? Most of us notice our physical appearance long before we become aware of our voice. This exercise awakens your vocal awareness. It's your first step to speaking like a pro.

Congratulations! You just gave a speech. Speaking is simply the act of talking. If you spoke your words in front of someone, you gave a public speech.

Public speaking is a skill like playing a sport, learning to dance or taking up a musical instrument. You get better at it the more you study it, practice it, play it, do it. And let's not forget that people do make asses out of themselves when they are in the process of learning.

Michael Jordan once said, "I've missed more than 9,000 shots in my career. I've lost almost 300 games. Twenty-six times I've been trusted to take the game-winning shot and missed. I've failed over and over and over again in my life. And that is why I succeed."

No matter what your dream is, the yellow brick road that leads you there is paved with effective verbal communication. If you learn to inform, persuade, entertain, motivate and inspire, you'll have to contend with fewer flying monkeys.

Yeah, but . . .

If we're going to get to the Emerald City, let's get the typical excuses out of the way before we go any further.

Excuse #1: I'm nervous!

If you're like most people, it doesn't take much for someone to blow you off in everyday conversation. You begin a sentence and before you finish it, someone jumps in with words you were going to say (maybe). You open your mouth and someone calls you out.

Doing the necessary work for a presentation, taking the risk of standing up before other people and talking and knowing that comments will be made—these considerations keep many of us frozen. Getting up from your seat and walking to a podium can seem like torture. Once you're there, your tongue ties into a knot, brain blips begin, and everyone in the audience looks like Simon Cowell.

My fear of speaking in front of an audience began in elementary school. I raised my hand to ask a question and was reprimanded for not paying attention to what the teacher had already covered.

Well, it may have been covered, but I sure didn't understand it. On occasion, other students would laugh at my questions. And when I did express my knowledge or opinion on a topic, I gave the resident bully more ammunition to fire at me.

Then there was the time I dressed up to give a presentation on Marie Antoinette. I had done the research, practiced out loud and was ready to launch my acting career.

Then my fifth-grade teacher said to the class, "I know you're all very nervous. I bet you can't breathe. You might even feel like you're going to die. Don't worry. You'll probably live!" After that introduction, I read my note cards in terror, stumbling from word to word, sounding like I was facing the guillotine.

This is the baggage you must leave behind.

But I can't, you say.

If that's how you feel, fine. But *act* like you can! *Pretend* you can! Remember how much fun make-believe used to be? It's time to bring that activity back into practice. Here's a well-kept secret: Pretending jump-starts reality.

Actors pretend. They learn to speak clearly and minimize the fear factor, using tools they have been taught, so they can be believable characters on camera and on the stage. If the actor does not learn to focus on his character and the needs of the listener, rather than on nervousness, his performance will suffer.

Like acting, public speaking requires specific skills that can be developed through exercises like the ones this book presents. The actor learns that through skill one can achieve art.

Throughout this book, I present many of the same exercises I studied at U.C.L.A. when I was getting my master's degree and later as an actor in New York. These useful techniques, which I learned through repeated practice, benefited me both onstage and off and turned me into a confident speaker.

These exercises are sometimes easy and sometimes not, but they are time-tested and audience-tested. They work. With each exercise, I will answer the question "Why?" and reveal its purpose, just as I did after the instructions in Exercise #1.

Doing each of these exercises, preferably more than once, will make you comfortable before an audience. Doing the exercises with excellence will make you feel better about yourself and increase your confidence.

Excuse #2: I'm just not the kind of person who likes drawing attention to myself.

Then pretend (there's that word again) you're just speaking one-on-one to a friend in need. Not to worry. We'll do several exercises to help with this one.

My pastor, who makes a public speech every time he gives a sermon, told me that he is shy by nature and outgoing by profession.

My cousin said that shyness is an excuse for not participating; it's easier to sit in the background and judge than it is to engage in conversation. It's so easy not to be shy when we're sitting behind our laptops or mobile devices.

It's time to remove that protective layer. Reach down—perhaps way down—and pull out the desire to become the best possible version of you and present it to others.

If you are shy, fine. But add *confident* to your self-description. Being confident means that you possess a positive attitude about what you can do and that you do not worry about what you can't do.

You can speak. Now open up your mouth and add some volume. You'll be amazed at how shyness fades into the background as you move to center stage.

Excuse #3: Speaking in front of an audience is easy for you. You're a natural.

I'm in good shape, and people say to me, "You're so lucky to be thin." Excuse me, but I'm out every morning for my four-mile walk, dance class or swim.

Try going to a driving range and hitting a golf ball for the first time. Good luck. It takes practice, study and a sense of humor. The same applies to opening your mouth and leaving your audience with that feeling in their gut that what you just said matters. That's a hole in one.

The chances for getting a hole in one get a whole lot better when you've researched the topic and practiced the presentation *out loud* many times.

Remember, 90 percent of luck is preparation.

This book makes preparation, practice and presentation a step-by-step process. That process takes time. We'll begin with the more comfortable speeches and work our way up to the challenging ones. I want you to feel good while you're following this process and relish how far you have come along the way.

When I was a size 20 and decided to lose weight, I bought an outfit in every size down to a 6. Going from a 20 to an 18 was a goal I could reach. And, wow, did I relish that 18 before moving on to getting into that 16 and eventually into that size 6.

Do the same with your public speaking journey—move along size by size, step by step, exercise by exercise.

Excuse #4: I'm never going to have a job where I have to give speeches.

Wrong. No matter what the profession, public speaking skills are required. And there's the job interview that precedes any job! Hello! A good resume, a strong academic background and a relative in the business might get you in the door for the interview, but what will get you the job is verbal communication, listening ability and enthusiasm.

If you choose to make public speaking a waste of time, it will be. If you choose to not get anything out of this book, you won't. If you choose to only *try*, that gives you an out for not succeeding.

Instead, as you read this book, jump in and don't let the words "I'll try" or "I can't" cross your lips. Do your best. As Yoda said, "Do or do not. There is no *try*."

Excuse #5: People will make fun of my accent!

This book was written by a Jersey girl. Hackensack! Hello! Ya know what I'm sayin'? I had an accent, but I knew that if I twalked like a character on *Jersey Shore*, my options for employment would be limited. Can you imagine Snookie as a speech instructor?

Getting rid of an accent is a controversial subject. I learned to tread lightly after a huffing and puffing fellow professor shoved a book in my face and declared, "Do you believe what I found in the library!?" The book was *How to Get Rid of Your Accent*. I heard, as did everyone else in the hallway at that moment, "This is racist!" I walked away with a fear of being tarred and feathered if I defended the book.

That professor declared modifying a strong accent out of bounds, yet I've come to believe strongly that doing just that is essential for clear and successful communication.

If there is any blockage to the flow of information—through an accent, in your attire, with the tone of your voice—as you speak to an audience, your message becomes less effective. That includes playing with your hair, walking around with your hands in your pocket, bobbing your head, tapping your fingernails—all of these, like an accent, are distractions from the message you want to convey.

What if a teacher walked into your history class carrying a purse and didn't put it down as she began her lecture? Not a big deal. But what if she continued to cling to that purse throughout the hour as she described the Battle of the Alamo? Would you be able to concentrate on what was said or would your focus be on that purse?

Yes, I got rid of my Jersey accent, unless I get really mad—then it returns with a vengeance. I concentrated on my choice of words, I slowed down my pace and became aware of the basics of enunciation, and my accent diminished. There's nothing wrong with an accent, but don't let it be a purse.

Excuse #6: I stutter.

Vice President Joe Biden has a stutter. So did Winston Churchill and Marilyn Monroe. I am not a speech therapist, but I do know what has worked for several students who have stood before a class and not been able to get out one sentence.

I had a student in my class whose stutter was not apparent until he stood up to give his first formal speech. As he began his introduction, he started to stutter. Soon he could not get one word out of his mouth. He was horribly embarrassed, but he stayed after class, and we worked out a schedule that started with him giving his speeches just to me.

We would meet before class. At first, I would keep the door closed. Then one day I left the door open and students began to filter into the classroom as he presented. I ignored the other students. I'm happy to report that my ignoring was contagious, and my student did the same, remaining completely focused on the purpose of his speech. He gave his final presentation before the entire class.

So, to start, you might need to give your speeches one-on-one with your teacher. Or you might want to begin by reading from your notes.

Absorbing what this book has to offer, being an active participant in your speech class and having a strong support team can give you the confidence to no longer be afraid of a stutter and thus to overcome it. If this sounds a tad epic, it is, especially if you've ever had a stutter.

Anyone who reads this book should see the movie *The King's Speech*, the story of Britain's King George VI, who with the help of an unconventional speech therapist overcomes a lifelong crippling stammer. At the film's end, George delivers a crucial radio speech to his British countrymen as they face their entry into World War II. It was through facing his own fear that the king found his voice and became a new man.

Excuse #7: I hate my teacher.

Then drop the class or find another teacher. If you don't trust the teacher, you won't listen to and receive her words of instruction nor will you act on them. You won't learn and improve.

If you are reading this book because you have been "forced" to or if you are taking a public speaking class simply because it is a requirement, you may be resistant to improving and growing.

Instead, please welcome this chance for self-improvement. Pretend that this book is a *New York Times* best seller. Pretend this class is one you have been looking forward to taking; be open to criticism and trust your instructor's comments.

Part of improving is being corrected by your teacher. Correction is probably one of the most difficult pills to swallow, especially when it is prescribed by another person.

Even when we have problems with a subject, we don't always recognize that we do, and we certainly don't want others to know we have them. That's another job a teacher must do—tell you that you're terrible when you are. It's also her job to tell you what works and what doesn't.

Seek teachers and friends who accept you not only for who you are but for who you can become.

Excuse #8: I hate to read.

That's okay. So do I.

The required reading in this book takes a backseat to exercises that provide the speaking time necessary for you to sound dignified and intelligent when you open your mouth.

Show, Don't Tell is a coach in book form.

If you were to make a choice between the book's exercises and the reading material, doing just the exercises would be much better than doing just the reading. Of course, I prefer you do both, but it's not my words that will make you someone who leaves an audience wanting more. Only the effort you put into the exercises will do that.

Excuse #9: I don't have time.

If we are going to get an education rather than just attend school, we are going to have to stay focused, because the world we live in is filled with distractions that gobble up our time.

You try to read this book and something else a great deal more interesting pops up. You try to practice, and the beep that announces a text speaks louder than your voice. Life provides distraction after distraction.

You have to learn—let's hope it's sooner rather than later—to say *no* to the continual orgy of distractions in our media-infused world. You have to turn them off when you read this book and do the exercises.

You have to be determined that nothing will hinder you from growing in this skill that you will utilize every day.

The mere thought of giving a speech can induce anxiety. To get past this feeling, turn down the pressure by taking baby steps. This book lays out those steps.

Excuse #10: Another book of rules!

Learn the rules first—then break them if you think it will improve your ability to give a good speech.

One rule you've heard since preschool is *Don't write in books.* Break it—if, of course, you own the book. Highlight what you think is most important. Write comments in the margins. Blog about your progress and post to http://thespeakingguide.com.

Here's one rule you should never break: Think before you speak. In fact, use the work *think* to help you qualify a thought as worthy of uttering aloud:

T	Is it true?
H	Is it helpful?
I	Is it inspiring
N	Is it necessary?
K	Is it kind?

Let's close this section with an exercise. It's cathartic—you'll feel five pounds lighter after you do it.

Exercise #2
Spitting It Out

Turn those cell phones back on. If you have a stop-watch app, start it.

Yell—and continue to yell for one minute.

If you don't have anything that's really bothering you, it's okay to yell as you describe what you did since you woke up this morning. Or yell out the ABCs over and over again. But don't stop for an entire minute.

If you want, call a friend and yell at him or her—after explaining that this is an exercise to improve your public speaking skills. Have your friend time you.

Why? Because I want you to hear yourself speaking loudly, and it comes much more naturally when you are venting. Have fun.

Chapter One:
Ready, Set, Yell

Confidence-Building Tools for Using Your Voice

Yell!

Again?

Yes.

This time we're not going to just vent. We're going to *concentrate* on venting. Concentration means focusing only on the task before us. We give our complete attention to what we are saying and doing.

I have attention deficit disorder. Yet while a bunch of kids are screaming and tearing apart an adjacent room, I have no problem concentrating on a conversation with other mothers. Nor do I have focus issues when I want to win an argument, even in a noisy restaurant. There are plenty of distractions in such scenarios, but I stay focused on my words.

This is the kind of focus you need when you give a speech. Without it, distractions will scream at you like a brat throwing a tantrum. Without single-minded attention on your message, clicking pens, loud whispers and text alerts can make your well-prepared presentation difficult to deliver.

When you direct your consciousness to where you want it to be, you stay on a clear course, and intrusions stay in the background, even if someone is in your face.

Here is an exercise I learned in a class on improvisation, the study of spontaneous presentation. It is an excellent way to learn to take and keep control of your thoughts and words.

Exercise #3
Concentration

Pair up with someone—a friend or family member, or a classmate. Now do exactly what you did in Exercise #2. Yell for one minute. Okay, you don't have to yell, but I find it very therapeutic to express myself loudly about something that's important to me. If you have nothing to vent about, let loose on every detail of your summer vacation. Or talk to me about what you're wearing or what your partner is wearing. If you run out of things to say, recite the ABCs or count to 50. Just don't stop talking for the next minute.

One more thing: Your partner in this exercise must yell, vent, tell, recite or count at the same time you are yelling, venting, telling, reciting or counting.

Stay focused on your words only. This takes concentration. And that concentration must last for one minute.

That's why the name of this exercise is not *yelling*, it is *concentration*. You must focus only on what you have to say and block out anything else the other person says.

Why? There will always be someone talking or something distracting going on while you give a speech. There is no quicker way than this exercise to learn to stop distraction in its tracks.

_____

The Most Important Part of Your Speech: The Slate

What is the slate? In the entertainment industry, it's your name. And you need to sound interested in it. If you don't sound interested in yourself, your audience has no reason to be interested in you.

When you slate your name, you need to say it in a way that shows how confident you are in yourself.

Presenting your slate is the most important part of a job interview or an audition, yet few speakers, job applicants or actors know how to do it properly.

When you walk up to a podium to begin a speech, if you have not been formally introduced, you say your name. When you walk into an office for an important interview, you shake hands and say your name. When you walk into a studio for an audition, the casting director points the camera at you and asks your name.

Big deal, we all know our names, you say. But knowing how to say your name determines whether your audience, potential boss or director will listen to the rest of what you have to say. Believe it or not, you can leave your audience wanting less rather than more just by the way you say your name.

Many people raise the pitch at the end when they say their names. Instead of keeping the sound on the same level—"Jeri Warren!"—they turn their name into a question—"Jeri Warren?"

Saying your name as though you're asking a question puts you in a position of weakness at a point when you should appear confident. What? You're asking a question? You don't know your own name?! Your name is a fact (unless you're thinking of changing it so it will look better on a marquee).

My name is Jeri Warren. I don't question it, and I'm happy with it.

You also must sound proud of your name. And you must say it slowly enough so that people get it the first time. If you need to repeat your name, you have said it too quickly, too quietly or too gloomily. You don't want to send a message that you are on a caffeine high, have laryngitis or have been dumped by your bff.

When I was an actress and went to auditions, I would walk onto a brightly lit stage, look into a dark theater and not be able to see the faces judging my every word. I was scared, so instead of focusing my attention on my nervousness, I pretended (there's that word again) that I was introducing myself to someone I really wanted to meet. I pretended to see a face before me, like Liza Minelli or Paul McCartney, and then I would say my name. Because I was concentrating on the person I imagined I was addressing, I had no time to feel nervous.

This was before I was married, and my maiden name was Niebergall. I am proud to say that not once was I asked to repeat my name. I was asked, "What kind of a name is that?" But I was not asked, "What was that, again?"

If you are about to give a speech and you are behind a podium, make sure you look at your audience when you proudly slate your name.

Eye contact is just as important as your slate. If you are introducing yourself to your potential boss, make sure you look at your potential boss. Eye contact is just as important as your slate. If you are slating to a camera at an audition, make sure you look into the camera and see someone who would be fun to meet. Eye contact is just as important as your slate.

I trust that by now you understand my point: Eye contact is very important.

Now let's move on to a speech that occurs very often in our daily lives.

How often are you out with a friend or acquaintance and you run into someone you know but your friend doesn't? If you forget about the person you're with, she stands there feeling like a fifth wheel while you chat with the other person. It's the better choice . . .

To Introduce

Introducing one person to another requires a small speech—one we need to give often and should be able to give easily.

Introductions and linking people up aren't just social courtesies but the best way to facilitate new relationships. The road to your future is paved through connections you make and other in-person networking. So it's important to know a few simple rules of etiquette for introducing people.

Start by naming the person who is most important to you first. For example, if I am with my husband and I run into a friend, I say, "Mark, I would like you to meet Pam." If you are introducing a high-ranking official or a member of the clergy, mention his or her name first: "Father Kilcoyne, I would like you to meet my husband, Mark." If you are introducing your boyfriend to your father, you'd better say, "Dad, this is Edward Cullen."

As you say each name, direct your eye contact back and forth from one person to the other.

Then there's that moment of silence after the initial introduction, so I generally throw in something about the second person named. "Mark, I would like you to meet Pam. Pam is a friend from work," or, "Dad, this is Edward Cullen. I think he might be a vampire."

If I am one of the people being introduced, I always shake hands, even if it's an informal introduction. Whether to shake hands is up to you, but if you do shake hands, no limp fishes, please! Your handshake is one of the first impressions you make. Be sure it is a firm one.

Whether or not you shake hands, even if you just say "hi" or "hey," make eye contact. If you don't make eye contact, you might as well be saying, "I could care less" or "I have no confidence in myself" or "Maybe there's someone else here who's way more worth my time than you are."

Then there's that really awkward moment when you don't remember the name of the person you want to introduce. My husband is well aware of the following cue: I say, "Oh, have you met my husband?" Then Mark says his name with the idea that the other person will do the same. Or you could just apologize and say you don't remember the other person's name.

Many of you may have difficulty or even feel embarrassed introducing people to one another and getting a conversation going. Get over it! Your fleeting moments of embarrassment will be worthwhile when someone compliments you for helping them socially or professionally. With some practice you can master the art of linking people up.

Exercise #4
The Introduction

Practice the following scenarios and do the intros. Make sure you offer a piece of information about the second person named.

> *You are with your grandmother and you run into a friend. (I don't care if you like your friend more; living to an old age is an achievement, so your grandmother should get the first reference, as should any family member.)*

> *You are with a friend and run into your boss. (If you want to score points with your boss, I would say his or her name first.)*

> *You are at a parent/teacher conference and you have to make the introductions.*

> *You are at work and your significant other comes to visit. Introduce a colleague.*

> *You have a friend over to work on a school project in your home and you introduce your family.*

> *You take your grandmother to church and introduce her to the pastor.*

> *You introduce your husband to your doctor.*

> *You introduce your friend to a Nobel laureate, Dr. Solbrig.*

> *You are with your boyfriend and you run into your ex-boyfriend. (Be careful with this one).*

Why? You should never exclude someone from a conversation by not taking the time to properly introduce him or her.

Shut Up & Listen

Great speakers are good listeners. We learn by listening, not by talking.

Listen to Howard Stern, Oprah Winfrey, David Letterman and Ellen Degeneres. Each one of them has made an art out of listening.

How do they do it? They give their full attention to their guests and make eye contact with them. They not only listen to their guests' words, but they show they are engaged. What is the result? A common reaction is a display of the heart as well as the funny bone.

You'll be amazed at how much you can learn about someone or something when you don't end a sentence for someone, don't interrupt and avoid reacting emotionally.

We learn through all the senses. Sound is just one, but it is a profound memory trigger as you study something new. I quickly learned my "five times" tables because of the way my second-grade teacher, Mrs. Riley, said them. The tone of her voice said I had no choice but to remember them. I also remember how the gentle, reassuring tone of my Algebra II teacher helped me achieve an A when I had failed Algebra I.

When you listen, you learn what is important to others and why. This will prove very useful when the time comes to choose a topic for a speech that will engage your audience. Effective listening will help increase the amount of information you learn and will decrease the amount of time you need to study that information.

When you listen effectively, you learn what works to keep the attention of your audience and what doesn't work. For example, the speaker who never gets to the point, who likes the sound of his own voice way too much or who doesn't know what he's talking about will lose his audience. Often this speaker doesn't even care or notice that this is happening.

Then there's the speaker who will leave his audience wanting more. He relates the topic to his audience, gets to his point and makes sure he delivers a few carefully researched examples in a succinct manner.

This is why it is so important to listen carefully to the presentations people make—a politician running for office, a teacher in a classroom, entertainers and others on television and radio, clergy and lay people in your place of worship. Attentive listening helps you learn what to do and what not to do when you are in front of an audience.

Pay attention to how you listen. Do you listen objectively? Do you listen for the facts, or are you carried along on the emotional response elicited by the speaker? Do you listen without judging? Do you listen for hidden meanings and for hints about what the speaker really means but isn't saying? Answering these questions will help you to prepare for how an audience will be listening when you are the speaker.

Listen to Charlie

Author and educator Charlie Sykes, that is. He wrote *Dumbing Down Our Kids*, which delivers a sobering report card on our educational system.

Here are a few personal observations about public speaking that made me take notice of Charlie Sykes. As I think about the speeches I've liked the least, I see some recurring characteristics:

- The speech is a pity party for the speaker.

- The speaker feels he deserves a good grade for just getting up in front of an audience and trying.
- The speaker is looking for only positive feedback and support to nurse her lack of self-esteem.

Speakers who make presentations that can be described like this need an attitude adjustment. They need to know about the "11 Rules Kids Will Not Learn in School." So I ask you to read, listen and ponder these words of wisdom from Charlie Sykes's book.

11 Rules Kids Will Not Learn in School

Rule 1: Life is not fair; get used to it.

Rule 2: The world won't care about your self-esteem. The world will expect you to accomplish something before you feel good about yourself.

Rule 3: You will not make $80,000 a year right out of high school.

Rule 4: If you think your teacher is tough, wait till you get a boss.

Rule 5: Flipping burgers is not beneath your dignity. Your grandparents had a different word for burger flipping; they called it opportunity.

Rule 6: If you screw up, it's not your parents' fault, so don't whine about your mistakes; learn from them.

Rule 7: Before you were born, your parents weren't as boring as they are now. They got that way paying bills, cleaning your room and listening to you tell them how idealistic you are. So before you save the rain forest from the blood-sucking parasites of your parents' generation, try delousing the closet in your own room.

Rule 8: Your school may have done away with winners and losers, but life has not. Some schools have abolished failing grades; they'll give you as many times as you want to get the right answer. This, of course, bears not the slightest resemblance to anything in real life.

Rule 9: Life is not divided into semesters. You don't get summers off, and very few employers are interested in helping you find yourself. Do that on your own time.

Rule 10: Television is not real life. In real life people actually have to leave the coffee shop and go to jobs.

Rule 11: Be nice to nerds. Chances are you'll end up working for one.

I include Charlie Sykes's "11 Rules" not to put anyone down. They are here to raise the bar.

When Your Speech Begins

You are about to give a formal speech. Do you know when it begins?

When you slate your name? That's the most important part of your speech, but it's not when it begins.

When you begin to talk about your topic? Those first thirty seconds are when you either grab your audience's interest in the topic or fail to do that, but it is not when your speech begins.

If you are in a class, and the teacher calls your name because it is your turn to present, or if you are a novice speaker who has just been called on at a community meeting—that's when your speech begins.

If you let out a sigh when you hear your name—which I have heard people do hundreds of times—the speech will often be as deflating as the sigh.

If you walk to the podium and make an excuse—announce that you just broke up with your boyfriend or just didn't have time to prepare, and flip your hair around for twenty seconds—your speech is definitely going to be mediocre. If you say to yourself or announce to the class that this speech is going to be awful, guess what? It will be awful.

My advice to you when you hear your name called is to shut up until you get to the podium and slate your name. Use this time of silence to simply breathe and be fully present in the moment.

And don't forget to look at your audience and be proud of your name when you slate it.

After the Slate

Take another breath to let your audience look at you and to allow yourself to look at your audience.

This is also the time when I concentrate on one of the four scenarios listed below so that the real beginning of my speech will not be just a warm-up to the body of the speech. When you move onto the opening of the speech—or from slate to copy, as it's called in show business—pretend one of the following:

- You are about to talk to someone who has a problem and you have the solution.
- You are about to present yourself as an authority on your topic.
- Something really great has just happened to you.
- You believe that what you're doing is important.

Oprah Winfrey once said something enlightening about her early days in television:

> *When I auditioned for my first TV job at nineteen, I had no idea what to do, so I pretended to be Barbara Walters. I'd sit like Barbara and I'd look down at the script and up at the camera because I thought that's how you act—all from what I had seen Barbara do. On the job, I started to forget to be Barbara sometimes and Oprah would start slipping through. But in the beginning, being Barbara was what saved me (Robert Barton, Acting Onstage and Off).*

Let's use a similar approach. Remove those awkward first moments of your speech by utilizing one of the four scenarios suggested above. They will help you show enthusiasm and/or compassion for your topic, and will help you show that you care. They will help you be a serious yet friendly authority on a subject. They will let your audience know you are delivering your speech from a place of knowledge.

Exercise #5
The Difference

Read the following paragraph out loud.

> *Robert Kennedy said, "There are those who look at things the way they are, and ask why? . . . I dream of things that never were, and ask why not?" Don't limit your dreams to what seems reasonable. Aim higher and do not be afraid to miss. Winston Churchill said, "Success is not final, failure is not fatal: it is the courage to continue that counts."*

Quotations are often part of a speech. When you do provide a quotation, bring a sense of aliveness to those words.

Now say the paragraph again, after you've chosen to enter a reality based on one of the four "pretend" scenarios presented above.

Why? To see and hear how much better you sound when you have a purpose.

_____

Ready, Set, Say

Okay, so you've yelled, concentrated, introduced and almost begun your speech. But if we can't understand what you're saying, you might as well text your message.

When I began to teach acting classes in California, Valleyspeak was rampant. The girls began every sentence with a crescendo of

"Oh my god!" Guys began their statements with "Dude." These students apparently did not realize that the mouth can open vertically—their jaws were always locked in a horizontal position when they spoke. I could not understand what they were saying.

When my son was a teen he had the ability to turn "I don't know" into a grunt. Nothing moved on his face. He communicated using only the back of his throat. I thought I was talking to Sylvester Stallone. I could not understand what he was saying.

It's very important to use your facial muscles, tongue and lungs when you speak. I need to understand what you are saying. Your teacher needs to understand what you are saying. Your audience needs to understand what you are saying!

One semester, a student was so soft-spoken that I could not hear him from two rows away. When I brought this to his attention, he said quietly, "Yeah, other teachers have told me that."

 "Then why didn't you take their advice? I need the same thing they needed—to hear your voice!" Can you tell I was more than a little ticked?

 "I don't know, I'm not that kind of person," he said.

I don't care what kind of person you are, we all need to be heard. That goes for every class, every teacher and every conversation.

Of the myriad sounds our bodies expel, only a select few are used for speech.

It's amazing that all the sounds of the English language are pronounced with outgoing breath. Your voice begins with breath, and we've come equipped with a massive muscle to get that breath out. So use it. Take some deep breaths and use them to power the sound of your voice. By the way, "person"—from the

Latin words *per* ("with" or "through") and *sonum* ("sound" or "voice")—is the root word for "personality." And no matter what your personality, you need to be heard *clearly*.

With diligent practice, that soft-spoken student not only found his voice but took on a stronger personality by semester's end.

In the theater, speaking clearly does not mean only speaking with bravado. The actor must speak loudly enough and with enough clarity to be heard and understood throughout the auditorium or classroom. Good projection is as much a matter of clarity as it is of sheer volume.

The audience needs to hear your words from start to finish. Mumbling is not an option. *Walkin'* is not a word. *Walking* is. *Ya* is not a word. *You* is.

There are five vowels in English: *a, e, i, o* and *u*. With the exception of *e*, speaking them requires movement of the lips and jaws.

When you see a *t* or a *d* at the end of a word, it is important that you say it. *Tha* is not a word. *That* is. *Wha* is not a word. *What* is.

When a word ends with *r*, don't say *ah*. It's *car*, not *cah*. It's *river*, not *riva*.

Taking the time to enunciate might slow you down a bit, but it will also give you time to think about what's coming out of your mouth before you put your foot into it. I saw a post that read, "Taste your words before you spit them out of your mouth." That is sound advice for all.

If you have an accent, listen to television personalities and news announcers. They have been trained to speak in a neutral accent and without local slang.

Tune in to Ellen Degeneres, Anderson Cooper and Stephen Colbert, and don't just take a look but also listen carefully. Not one of their words is slurred, mumbled or dropped. And note that they never introduce themselves or any of their guests with a question mark at the end of a name.

Sofia Vergara of *Modern Family* has an accent, but you can hear all of her words clearly because she slows her pace and enunciates her words for her audience.

Your mouth and your words will fully awaken in the next exercise. Slurred, mumbled or dropped words? Not when you master the following.

Exercise #6
Watch Out, Shakespeare

Go to the front of the class or into a large room or step outside to read the verses that follow. Stand or sit up straight so you can open up those pipes of yours.

It is important that you read the following verses *out loud* and with a bit of drama. Open your mouth when saying each word. Don't forget to pronounce your *t*'s and *d*'s at the end of a word, even though at the start you may think you are over-pronouncing them.

If you don't know the correct pronunciation of a word, ask your teacher or go to Dictionary.com.

If you're reading in front of a class, take just one of the paragraphs. If you are alone, pretend you are in front of 50 people. Project to the person farthest away from you.

Speak *slowly*. Your jaw and mouth need time to fully open.

Start reading.

> The actuary's honorary secretary showed her
> extraordinary literary superiority by working literally
> solitarily in the library particularly regularly during
> February.

> With blade, with bloody blameful blade,
> he bravely broached his boiling bloody breast
> amidst the mists and coldest frosts
> with barest wrists and stoutest boasts.

Peter Piper picked a peck of pickled peppers,
a peck of pickled peppers Peter Piper picked.
If Peter Piper picked a peck of pickled peppers,
where's that peck of pickled peppers Peter Piper picked?

She sells sea shells on the sea shore,
The shells she sells are sea shells for sure.
If she sells sea shells on the sea shore
I'm sure she sells seashore shells.

Little Italy literally
Literally little Italy
Little Italy literally
Literally little Italy
Little Italy literally
Literally little Italy

Julia was actually due to be married to the Duke of Turin
on the first Tuesday in June, dressed in her superb jewels.
When the day duly arrived, Julia's mature duenna could
not produce the jewels. Julia felt suicidal, for the Duke,
pursuant to his promise, had dutifully started a ducal
serenade with a superfluous but celestially tuneful Tudor
tune played on lutes and flutes.

As I went into the garden
I saw five brave maids
Sitting on five broad beds
Braiding broad braids.
I said to these five brave maids
Sitting on five broad beds
Braiding broad braids,
"Braid broad braids, brave maids."

I thought a thought.
But the thought I thought wasn't the thought
I thought I thought.
If the thought I thought I thought had been
The thought I thought, I wouldn't have thought so much.

Betty bought a bit of bitter butter,
But the bit of bitter butter Betty bought was too bitter,
So Betty bought another bit of bitter butter
To make her bit of bitter butter better.

Something in a thirty-acre thermal thicket of thorns
And thistles thumped and thundered threatening
The three-D thoughts of Matthew the thug.
Although, theatrically, it was only the thirteen-thousand
Thistles and thorns through the underneath of his thigh
That the thirty-year-old thug thought of that morning.

Why? To perfect rhythm, spacing and pronunciation. On the other side of discomfort lies mastery.

Chapter Two:
The Road to Showing, not Telling:

Empower Your Words Through Demonstration

Your journey along this road does not begin with "I can't" or "I'll try." Neither of those subject/verb configurations is permitted in my classes. If you say, "I can't," it means you will not step out of your comfort zone. If "I'll try" is your mantra, you open the door to failure. Instead, say to yourself, "Just do it."

You can change your course of action, accelerate your growth and modify your behavior, but to do so you must first reorient your thinking. There is creativity inside each of us that must be tapped into without fear of failure.

Often we find ourselves in a rut. We do the same thing, bitch about the same people and circumstances and then say we're bored with life because we are afraid to do something different.

Instead, travel a road that diverges from the norm.

First, an evaluation: Where are you along the road to becoming a better communicator? You are in a good place if:

> You move from your seat to the podium without a sigh, moan or excuse.

You slate proudly and without turning your name into a question.

Your voice reflects that you speak with confidence and authority.

You take the time to pronounce your words so others can understand you.

Now you are almost ready to begin your speech.

As I've said from the beginning, the more you are in front of an audience the more comfortable you will be, and improvisations—which require no preparation time—can be done, with or without an audience, many times during a typical afternoon or evening.

Improvisation is one of the most important tools for building confidence in front of an audience. It requires the participants to tap into the creativity that we all possess. There is no better way to learn to be creative and to speak than by doing improvs. Let's combine the next exercise, on improvisation, with your newfound enunciation skills.

Exercise #7
Improve with Improv

Speak for a minute on one of the following topics. No prep time, just do it.

Better yet, do several. Have someone else, like your teacher, choose the topic. Remember, you must engage that person in the last row.

> Taking an exam
> Winning a prize
> Falling and breaking an arm
> Watching my favorite television show
> Brushing my hair
> Getting caught in the rain
> Getting to school late
> Playing a game of checkers
> Watching the sunset
> Eating dinner
> Washing the dishes
> Going to school

Why? To combine your improvisation skills with your enunciation abilities.

You are now ready to begin your demonstration, informative, persuasive or motivational speech.

Remember: It's key to engage your audience in your topic in the first thirty seconds. If you don't, people in the audience will begin looking at their fingernails or cell phones, which have become more intriguing than you as a speaker and what's coming out of your mouth.

If you sit down to read a novel, the first few pages had better be interesting in order for you to continue to turn pages. If you go to a movie, the first five minutes must grab you so you don't sneak into another theater. If you haven't done damage to something within seconds of beginning a new video game, don't you long for Grand Theft Auto?

There is no time for a warm-up when you give a speech, either.

I use a trick to make sure I am engaged with my audience from the beginning. After I slate my name, I take a moment to imagine I hear a friend ask a question about my topic. It gives me time to take a breath and collect my thoughts.

Before I give a demonstration speech on how to make the perfect omelet, I hear a friend ask, "What do your kids like to eat for breakfast?" When I give an informative speech on how to go to college for free, before beginning I hear in my mind the son of my neighbor, saying, "I'm not a trust fund kid, my cumulative is 2.4 and I'm not a jock! How can I afford to go to college?"

No, I am not crazy and I don't hear strange voices in my head telling me to do things. I simply *choose to pretend* to hear someone ask me a question.

Once I hear the question, the focus is off me and on the question, and voilà, I've minimized my nervousness. When a friend asks you a question, are you nervous? When a friend needs your help and you've been there, done that, would you keep your knowledge a secret?

Let's get you presenting, again, this time with an extemporaneous speech. Like the improvisation, this speech is delivered with little or no preparation. It asks the presenter to use background knowledge and experience.

Every time you are called upon to answer a question in class, you speak extemporaneously. For this exercise, I will also ask you to hear the question before you speak as though it is being asked by someone you care about.

Exercise #8
Quotations to Remember or Not

Words have power. What we say affects others. How have words affected you? Think about the words of advice that your parents have passed down to you and that you carry with you and probably will think about for your entire life.

Quotations are a great addition to any speech. When you quote, make sure to give credit where credit is due; always say who said it.

What about something a teacher told you? Or something you read? What's your favorite song lyric?

Explain to your audience what these words of advice mean to you and how they have affected your actions. Make sure you have a beginning, a middle and an end to your extemporaneous presentation.

Before you begin, hear the question that best applies to your extemporaneous delivery.

Why? Because words have power. Bring home to your audience how the words you've chosen have either made you stumble or moved you forward. Plus, familiarity with extemporaneous speaking helps reduce stage fright.

_____

People often tell me they don't know what topic to demonstrate, what idea to promote. In every speech that you will ever give, you must fill in the blank at the end of this sentence:

> I want to leave my audience with a better understanding of _____.

In my demonstration speech, I want to leave my audience with a better understanding of how to make the perfect omelet.

In my informative speech, I want to leave my audience with a better understanding of how to get college scholarships and grants.

If you can fill in that all-important blank, you will be able to come up with a topic. You will also know where you are going in your speech. As Alice in Wonderland said, "If you have no idea where you are going, how will you know when you get there?"

Now you are ready to start your speech. You have thought about your presentation, but you have yet to start your speech.

The Demonstration Speech

This is going to be simple and fun—all you need is something to demonstrate.

Tune into 50 percent of cable channels and someone will be demonstrating something.

Rachael Ray and Martha Stewart make millions demonstrating. YouTube and Pinterest are how-to buffets for the knowledge-hungry.

The aim is to teach an audience how something works or how to do something. Choose something physical that you can put your hands on—a tie, a snowplow, a skateboard, a basketball, a diaper, a guitar, anything!

Ask yourself seven questions to help you narrow down your choices as you decide what and how to demonstrate:

1. Do listeners really need to see the process to understand it?

Unless you are demonstrating to a two-year-old, forget about showing how to make a peanut butter and jelly sandwich. We all got this by the time we were three. We also know how to button a shirt, tie our shoelaces and brush our teeth. In other words, don't talk down to your audience with simplistic subjects. Don't demonstrate how to make a boxed cake when all you have to do is add water. Do we need to demonstrate how to add water? I hope not.

Show an audience your skill at something they might want to try or will need to know in the future—like how to tie a tie or how to perform CPR.

Show us how to make your grandmother's homemade lasagna, your mother's Uruguayan fruit salad or your own recipe for chocolate-chip-peanut-butter-cream-cheese brownies.

2. Is the subject limited enough to be demonstrated in the allotted time?

In other words, don't demonstrate origami. When a student attempts this demonstration, the speech lasts for way longer than the audience can bear. Sure, the speaker might be able to make a crane, but most of his audience will have crumpled their paper into a ball by the fifth fold.

Choose a topic that can be demonstrated within a set time frame—ten minutes tops, but nothing so simplistic that it takes less than three minutes. This is an A.D.D. nation, so K.I.S.S your audience.

K	Keep
I	It
S	Short (and)
S	Simple

3. Are the steps of the process clear, concise and in proper sequence?

Will you leave your audience with a better understanding of how something works or how to do something by the end of your speech? If you are demonstrating hip-hop moves, you will need to get your audience moving. No one learns to dance by watching, and your audience must be viewing you from behind so that they have the right perspective on your movements and are on the right foot even though they have two left feet.

If you are demonstrating a recipe, you need to have all your ingredients pre-measured. On a table, line up containers of the ingredients—Morton Salt, Calumet Baking Powder and Land-O-Lakes Butter, plus an egg container—but be sure they don't block the audience's view of the demonstration area.

Then, step by step, pull out the pre-measured ingredients from behind the containers and put them together in the correct sequence and using the right techniques. Place the mixture in the proper container for heating or refrigeration.

Finally, show the finished product with a dash of tah-dah! and hand out samples to the audience.

If your process has more than five steps, group the steps into categories. For a demonstration titled "How to Create a Longboard Setup," here's a reasonable template:

I. The first step is to choose the longboard that fits your needs.
    A. Downhill for speed
    B. Free ride for jumps, slides and tricks
    C. Tech slide for high-speed slides
II. The second step is to equip the board.
    A. You will need grip tape (SHOW IT)
    B. You will need trucks (SHOW IT)
    C. You will need wheels (SHOW IT)
    D. You will need bearings (SHOW IT)
III. The third step is to assemble the board.
    A. Apply grip tape to the top of longboard (DO IT)
    B. Place bearings in wheels (DO IT)
    C. Attach wheels to trucks (DO IT)
    D. Fasten trucks to deck (DO IT)

4. Are you well-rehearsed with what you will demonstrate?

You need to be an authority on the topic. Don't demonstrate how to tie a tie if your mother has done it for you all your life. Don't demonstrate how to make cookies if you don't know the difference between baking powder and baking soda.

One of my students wanted to demonstrate how to tie toe shoes. I knew the student was an amateur because, in the dance world, "toe shoes" don't exist; they are called "pointe shoes."

In other words, be well-trained in what you demonstrate. But remember that you can become well-prepared in how to tie that tie or make that apple- pumpkin smoothie within hours.

You must keep your demonstration as mistake-free as possible. Then again, on more than one occasion television chef Julia Child made mistakes while demonstrating her recipes. When she did, she simply laughed at herself, took a sip of cooking sherry and moved on.

5. Are your visuals visible?

I can't see how you tie that tie if I am in the back row of a classroom or if you are facing me and everything you do is backward. The answer? Go to Salvation Army and get a bunch of 50-cent ties, or raid your father's closet and pass them out to the class. Then make sure that the class is either standing alongside you and at least facing the same direction that you face as you demonstrate.

6. Is your demonstration silence free?

Your actions and your words should be coordinated. If you are demonstrating how to cook the best brownies in the world, you should have all the ingredients pre-measured. Show your audience that you have to add flour (and put the pre-measured flour into the mixing bowl), softened butter (and put the pre-measured softened butter into the mixing bowl) . . . and the process continues.

As you put the ingredients in the bowl and stir them into batter, you can't have what is called dead airtime. If there is more than a three-second pause in your speech as you place, stir or whatever, guess what? You'll lose your audience. Fill in dead airtime with a mention of the kind of flour you use or why it is important that you soften the butter. All of this must be done while you remain focused on your audience, not on the product.

7. Someone in your audience doesn't like brownies and could care less if he knows how to make them. What are you going to do about that attitude?

Never begin a speech, any speech, with "I'm going to talk to you about X."

Never begin any speech with "I'm going to tell you how to make brownies." Share a story instead. Show me why this brownie recipe is special to you.

For one brownie recipe speech, my student introduced her topic with, "I hated elementary school. I'm not too thrilled with high school. But I do like going home and seeing my grandmother, who lives with us. Lots of times we'll just sit and talk and she listens. Sometimes we sit and talk over the homemade brownies she makes. They're the best, and I'd like to share the recipe with you."

One of my favorite speech introductions was to a demonstration speech titled "How to Make a Paper Airplane." The speaker began, "Imagination is one of the most important parts of being a child. The ability to entertain yourself and turn nothing into something is what makes a kid a kid. Although everyone has an imagination, not everyone exercises it. Here was one of my favorite ways to do it—making paper airplanes." The speaker showed us some of his more elaborate creations, then demonstrated and had his audience members make one that had just six folds.

A story is a great way to begin a speech because it gets your audience emotionally involved. That being said, not everyone in your audience is going to like you or what you're talking about, even if you stand on your head and spit nickels. But never let them curb your enthusiasm. Be understanding and gracious, and move forward.

Make continual eye contact. Focus on the friendly faces in the audience and don't pay attention to the people who are yawning or looking out the window. Look at one positive face at a time and talk to that one. If all goes well, that reaction will be supportive, which will add to your confidence. Notice I said "adds to your confidence," not "gives you confidence." You are the one who is in control, not the people in the audience.

Details Matter

Even if you follow all seven suggestions discussed above, you can still ruin a perfectly good speech by using the wrong verb form or inappropriate language and or by the inflection of your voice.

Watch Your "Go," "Drink" and "Do"

One way to lose credibility as a speaker is to use an incorrect verb form.

Wrong verb forms are as grating on the nerves as nails scratching on a chalkboard. "Go," "drink" and "do" blunders are the biggest culprits.

You *go* if you're in the present; you *went* if you did something in the past. If you throw *have* into the equation, you're in the past perfect and you *have gone*. In other words, there are three forms to every verb. Get them right.

A simple sentence often used as an excuse is, "I should have drank less." When I hear that my inner siren shrieks through my bulging eyes. We *drink* today. We *drank* yesterday. We *should have drunk* less.

I asked someone for directions when I was totally lost in the subway and was told, "What ya shoulda did was . . ." I know, I know, I should be thankful he helped me, but this is just an example. There's that understood *have* when he said *shoulda* (*should have*) before the verb, so go with the third form of the verb: "What ya shoulda done."

Listed below are just a few verb forms. For an extended list of irregular verbs, see Appendix A at the end of the book. Please look at them, then memorize them. If you don't need to, because you already know them, thank your English teacher. Most dictionaries also give the three forms of verbs.

Present	Past	Past Perfect
go	went	gone
drink	drank	drunk
do	did	done
see	saw	seen
bring	brought	brought
write	wrote	written
break	broke	broken
drive	drove	driven
throw	threw	thrown
get	got	gotten

I recommend that you have a copy of *The Elements of Style* by Strunk and White at your side whenever you write a paper or prepare to give a speech. No book, using fewer words, is a better crash course in basic English composition skills. These skills are a must when you need to sound like an authority on a topic.

Watch Your Mouth!

Also watch your mouth when it comes to four-letter words (you know the words and their variations I refer to). They are never appropriate in a speech. Speeches are not given for the speaker, but for the audience. Any audience will stop taking you seriously as soon as you start using such words. No exceptions.

Watch Your Inflection

Don't turn sentences into questions when they are not questions. That is, avoid the temptation to raise your voice at the end of sentences.

This is the same idea as not turning your name into a question when you are introducing yourself. Don't make this mistake with your sentences either—unless, of course, you are asking a question.

Giving a Successful Demonstration Speech

Have you asked yourself the seven questions presented on pages XXX–XXX to help you choose what and how to demonstrate? Have you brushed up on your verb forms, cleared your speech of any bad language, and trained yourself to not say a declarative sentence as though it's a question?

If so, it's time to . . .

- Decide on your opening story, the part of your speech that will get the audience's attention.
- Present your demonstration—if necessary, using the template provided after Question #3.
- Decide how you will close your speech.

Finally, practice your speech—out loud. You do not give your speech in your head, but practice it audibly, *aloud,* ***out loud!***

Exercise #9
The Demonstration

It's time to do this in front of the class. Or if you're going this alone, deliver it in person or even Skype it to a friend. Again, it's always good to have at least one friend who accepts you not only for who you are, but also for who you can become.

Give your demonstration speech.

Why? Because it will help you learn to present the best version of yourself and encourage someone to try what you just demonstrated, thus making that person a happier, healthier and more fulfilled human being! Do I hear an *amen*?

_____

After the demonstration presentation, I ask my students how they felt before and after the speech. Most *before* answers are variations on the "sick to my stomach with nerves" theme. As much as we try to avoid it, pressure is inevitable, so learning to deal is a life skill we need to possess. Most *after* answers reflect a sense of accomplishment.

I would like to throw in a *bravo!* to all those who gave their demonstrations without excuses.

Demonstration Speech Checklist

Before we continue on to the next chapter, let's take a moment to see how you think you did in Exercise #9: The Demonstration.

Become your own observer and look at your speech from the point of view of your audience. Being as objectively honest as you can be, grade your speech as you think audience members might.

1. Was your introduction an attention grabber?

Did you begin your speech from the moment you got up from your seat and walked to the podium? Did you look at your audience when you slated your name? Did you take a breath and hear the question you silently asked yourself?

For your intro, did you avoid saying "What I'm going to talk to you about"? Instead, did you lead with a story or interesting fact that revealed why you wanted to share this demonstration with your audience?

2. Did you appear interested in what you were talking about?

If you weren't, your audience probably wasn't.

3. Did you show why the audience should listen to you?

Did you reel in the audience with a good story about how you made an ugly rooftop into a place of beauty, even if they didn't care about gardening? Did you give the audience a reason to listen to what you had to say? Did you show your enthusiasm so that the audience would follow you?

4. Did you state your main points clearly?

Did you finish in the allotted time—usually no more than ten minutes—with simple, clear steps that even a mind that's half-consumed with planning weekend activities could follow?

5. Did your use of visuals or other props appear well rehearsed?

Were you able to keep your focus mainly on your audience, have no dead airtime and appear adept at handling your props?

6. Did you project?

Did you project with your voice so all could hear you—down to your word endings? Did you also project a positive attitude?

7. Did you inspire listeners to do something they would not have done before the speech?

If I you think at least some in the audience will go home and cook that brownie recipe that is so much better than anything store-bought, then you've given a good demonstration speech.

8. Did you use proper grammar?

Or did you say that there bad stuff like "What ya shoulda did"?

9. Did you explain words and terms the audience might not understand?

10. Did you provide an appropriate ending?

Hopefully, you didn't end with, "Well, that's it." Did you instead suggest that audience members go home and try what you just demonstrated or enjoy what you made? Or did you refer back to your opening story, another satisfying type of conclusion?

11. Did you present the best version of you?

12. Did you leave your audience wanting more?

Exercise #10
Index Card Almighty

Get an index card. It will make a great bookmark and reminder.

On the front, write down three things you think you did well during your demonstration speech. The Demonstration Speech Checklist can help you see the strengths you showed in your speech.

Again, trying to be objective, on the back write down three things you think need improvement.

Why? You'll use this index card as a reminder of what needs to change and what needs to remain the same as you prepare to give your next speech.

_____

Chapter Three:
Break a Leg

Making It Easy for Your Audience to Receive Your Information

In the theatrical world, people say, "Break a leg" before an actor goes onstage to perform. It's another way of saying, "Good luck." No one says "Good luck" before a show because saying it is bad luck.

A broken mirror is seven years bad luck. People carry a rabbit's foot for good luck. If you aced your demonstration speech with little preparation—that's luck!

It's more likely that the successful outcome of your first formal presentation was proportional to the amount of thought and practice you put into it. For the majority of us, when it's time to give a speech, it's not about luck; it's about preparation.

To put it another way: Luck is preparation.

Most of us are guilty of procrastination. We wait until it is too late to take advantage of the time available to prepare with a level head and without anxiety. The first rule of being prepared: Set up a schedule for your work and stick to it instead of putting things off until the last minute.

Public speaking is a learnable skill, but it takes practice. If you commit to doing the exercises in this book, you will develop your speaking abilities. You will also have an enormous advantage even in an extremely competitive job market.

I hope that in your first presentation you shared with your audience a passion or a concern and that you used that demonstration to improve the audience's understanding. I hope your audience remembered you not just for the information you delivered, but for the relationship you had with them. If you were more concerned about you and how you felt, it's likely your audience was less concerned about you and what you showed them. You need to show concern for your audience.

Liza Minnelli gave the greatest acting tip I have ever heard.

> *It's not the how it's the why.*

What does this have to do with giving a speech?

It's always evident when someone gives a speech just because it is an assignment. Okay, many speeches are given because of an assignment at school or a requirement at work, but it should never come off that way. *How* you do something reflects your preparation, but your delivery shows *why* you do it. The *why* shows your audience whether you care and whether you are worth their time.

Moving Down the Path Toward the Informative Speech

I find that my students' apprehension about giving a speech begins with not knowing what topic would be of interest to them or to their audience. It's easy to outline, easy to use a template, but not so easy to choose what to outline or plug into that template.

In most classes you're told what your writing assignment is. Maybe that's why something that should be a welcome change— the need to choose your own topic—becomes a worry. Why not use that worry to come up with a topic for your informative speech? For example:

> The Effects of Anxiety on the Body
> Ways to Relieve Tension
> The Saving Power of Yoga

If you couldn't care less, that's fine. Choose something else.

> Why School Is Boring
> What Is Teen Angst?
> A Brief History of Your Favorite Team or Event or Custom

If you're tempted to put selecting your topic off to another day, that's fine. Make that day Idea Day—a day when you open your mind to receive new ideas.

You can do anything that day: Go to the library or a bookstore. Go to a museum or a beach. Try sushi. Take in a movie. Read *Rolling Stone* magazine. Think about where you would like to travel or what unique experiences you have had or would like to have. On Idea Day, do only things that will keep you open to your creative ability. Those things are different for everyone, so explore!

In other words, tap into your feelings. See where they lead, and see if along the way you find a speech topic. But don't wait for the day before the speech is due to have your Idea Day. Do it when you first get the assignment.

You're not writing a master's thesis—that decision is very involved and requires a committee to approve your topic. My thesis was "A Study of the Career of Gwen Verdon" and was 115 pages long. Because you have five to ten minutes to give your speech, anywhere from two to five main points about your subject will be plenty.

Yet I could easily convert my 115-page thesis into a five- to ten-minute informative speech. "How Gwen Verdon Changed Broadway" narrows the topic and could be covered in the allotted time. Yes, I could talk about Gwen Verdon for hours, but I can get two to five informative points about her across in a few minutes if I concentrate on a single facet of her career.

In the demonstration speech, you showed me how to do something. Your hands were on an object as you assembled, stirred, created and displayed your skill. When you give a speech to inform, you describe and explain; in this case, your hands don't play such an important role.

As a way of narrowing your topic, say to yourself, "I want to leave my audience with a better understanding of . . ."

> "I want to leave my audience with a better understanding of Gwen Verdon's talent."

> "I want to leave my audience with a better understanding of my Grand Cayman vacation."

> "I want to leave my audience with a better understanding of remedies for insomnia."

Remember, make the decision about what you will share with your audience as soon as you get the assignment. This will give you time to research and practice. That being said . . .

Watch Out for Eye Crack! Yes, It's Out There.

Beware the evil temptation to read your speech. This slippery slope can begin, innocently enough, with the urge to write out your speech. Or maybe you want to take that English or American history paper that got you an A and make that your speech.

You look through the paper. Yes, you think. This is good, and if I got a good grade on the paper, I will surely get a good grade on my speech. On top of that, think of all the time I'll save on researching—it's already done. So you latch onto that paper. You carry it to the podium when it's time to present your speech. Next stop: rock bottom, as your eyes remain fixed on that paper as you read your speech verbatim to the audience.

Hello! This is public speaking, not public reading. You *must not* read your speech word for word from a piece of paper.

As soon as you write your speech out word for word, as though you are writing an English essay, you run the risk of reading your speech from the hard copy rather than presenting it. You will need to convert your material from paper form into one of several outline forms.

When you create an outline, you *cannot* read your speech.

The way you read something is very different from the way you speak in conversation. You are learning public speaking, not public reading.

Yes, I know, the President of the United States reads his speeches verbatim, but he's got a transparent teleprompter that allows him to remain focused on his audience.

Any walls between you and your audience must be broken down, even if that wall is as thin as a piece of paper. If you take an essay to the podium instead of an outline, your eyes become glued to the paper and you can't pull them away.

Does the teacher who reads from a text during class hold your attention? How awful are those radio commercials where you can tell that every word is read off a script? A speech is not a recitation.

Presentations must be designed to get the audience involved. If you want to have any kind of relationship with your audience and if you want them to walk away with at least some knowledge of what you have been talking about, then do not read your speech.

Of course, it is sometimes necessary to read parts of a book, a paper or other notes during a speech, but do so for only a few seconds. And here's a valuable tip: Whenever possible, instead of looking down to read, put the words you must read into a visual and read from that. Then your audience can see as well as hear the words you speak. That's better than having the audience stare at the crown of your head while you read your notes.

If you hafta, hafta, hafta write your speech out completely, go ahead. But then turn it into an outline, and throw out the written-out version after you've created the outline.

I hope I have made this point very clear: You need to *create an outline and present your speech from that outline.*

The Thesis Statement

Before you can begin to make an outline you must have a clearly defined thesis statement—the main topic or main argument that you will talk about. It will eventually become part of your outline, but you must decide on a thesis statement first.

A thesis statement is not the first sentence you utter when you deliver the speech. It is the first sentence you write when you outline the speech. It is *the topic of your speech in sentence form.*

In order to write a valid thesis statement, you must do the following:

Be declarative. State what you are going to say in the overall speech. Do this with a simple sentence that narrows your topic to two to five main points. A good way to make this sentence declarative is to state that simple sentence framed by words or phrases like *today, this afternoon* or *my purpose.*

Enumerate. An audience can't follow more than five points. "Today I will give you four reasons for outlining a speech." Or "The purpose of today's speech is to show you three ways to train your cat." This sets up a preview of the speech. If an audience knows how many points are coming, it is easier for them to comprehend the points as you lay them out and connect them during the speech.

Be specific. Never use the words *on, about* or *discuss.* "My speech is on . . ." is about as bad as it gets. Such words allow you to speak very generally and with no clear purpose. You need a specific purpose, and you need to declare that purpose so an audience knows where to focus. "Today I am going to talk about education" leaves an audience with no clue because education is a very broad topic. On the other hand, like it or not, tests are key components in our educational system. The thesis statement "This afternoon I will address three things you need to do in order to ace a test" narrows your topic to a specific element of education that you can cover in the time available.

Design your thesis statement for public acceptance. Don't alienate your audience by sounding arrogant, stupid or unprepared. If you do, they won't listen to the rest of your speech. A snowboarder began his speech with video footage of his downhill expertise. It was impressive, but when the video was over, he said with a nod, "Yeah, I know. Awesome!" His ego trumped any of the words that followed.

When we speak, the audience has one chance to get clear on what we are saying. The thesis statement is their key to understanding the speech. Follow the rules given above for this sentence and the most difficult part of creating your outline is over.

The Classic Outline

In preparing the outline for your speech, you can go with the classic outline you learned in English class:

I. Introduction. Begin with a question, story, statistic, picture or quotation that gets the attention of your audience and involves them in the topic. Show them your enthusiasm for the purpose at hand.

II. Thesis Sentence. Be declarative. Enumerate. Be specific. Design for public acceptance.

III. Body of the Speech. The body consists of two to five main points that relate back directly to the thesis. Categorize all your information into these points. Make each main point as important as any other main point.

    A. First Main Point

        1. Subpoint (can use an example, statistic, quotation, fact)
        2. Subpoint (same as above)

B. Second Main Point

    1. Try for the same number of subpoints . . .
    2. . . . as in the first main point.

IV. Conclusion. Keep it short. The conclusion tells the audience the finale of your speech is coming. Summarize the main points and tie them to the thesis, leaving your audience with no doubt about the purpose of the speech.

    A. Summary of main points (tied to the thesis)
    B. Final statement (more on this below)

Exercise #11
Pet Peeve

Planning a speech on one of your pet peeves is a great way to sharpen both your outlining and presentation skills.

What makes you mad? Use the template below to get your thoughts in order. When you know what you're going to say and are ready to present your vent, *do not read your notes.*

1. Introduction. Begin with a story that sets up what your pet peeve is.

> I was on a blind date. The guy was good-looking, had a nice car and was a great conversationalist, and he took me out to dinner at The Four Seasons. When the food arrived, he continued to speak while he chewed it.

2. Thesis Statement. Then say what your pet peeve is.

> Speaking and chewing don't mix, and I find it disgusting. I have one more incident I would like to share with you that amplifies my point.

3. Body of Speech. Give one more story about why this is your pet peeve.

> It was during Thanksgiving dinner. Everyone in my family talks at once, and my little sister loves to be the center of attention. So what did she do? She screamed her words, and consequently not only her words but her food blurted out.

4. Conclusion. End on the upbeat. State what has or could be done to lessen the pain of this pet peeve.

There is nothing I can do about my sister wanting to be the center of attention, but I no longer sit next to her at the dinner table. And that blind date I had? When he called me for another date, I actually got up the nerve to tell him how grossed out I was by his lack of table manners. Haven't heard from him, again. And that's a good thing.

Why? Why not take one more step closer to speaking like a pro?

More Thoughts on the Outline Template

Even when a speech is short, like the pet peeve speech discussed above, the audience must able to understand you and be compelled by what you say. The classic outline helps you achieve these goals.

As you prepare the outline for your speech, you will ask yourself a series of questions. Keep these questions in your head, but do *not* include them in your speech:

- What is the title of my speech?
- What is the purpose of my speech?
- How will I open the speech to get my audience's attention?
- What is my statement of purpose?
- What two to five main points do I want to make?
- What examples, anecdotes, humor, statistics, quotations or other information will support my main points?
- How can I entertain the audience?
- How can I summarize briefly what I have said to make my audience remember my main points?
- How will I close my speech?

The first two questions are not part of the presentation of your speech, but they are an essential part of clarifying your thoughts. If your thoughts are not clear, concise and to the point, the audience will not know where you are going and will not want to follow you.

What is the title of my speech?

The title sums up the speech, as a movie title does. *Legally Blonde* tells the tale in two words. It says what it is. So do *Knocked Up*, *Nightmare on Elm Street* and *Hangover*.

What does the title of a movie have to do with my speech? If you can't tell me in a title what your speech is about, then you can't tell me what your speech is about in ten minutes either. A good title helps you narrow your subject. "A Study of the Career of Beyoncé" does not do this. "Beyoncé's Talent" does.

Show me specifically the path you will take and sum it up with the title. You generally do not share the title of your speech with your audience. This title is for your benefit.

What is the purpose of my speech?

In other words, I want to leave my audience with a better understanding of _____. How you fill in the blank is not to be shared with your audience. This blank is for your benefit; it helps with the formation of your thesis statement.

How will I open the speech to get my audience's attention?

This is where the verbal speech presentation begins. Know whom you will speak to. Don't talk down to your listeners or use a reference to which they cannot relate. I'm a believer in stories. You can also use an illustration, a startling fact or statistic, a quotation or humor, or you can ask a question.

If you ask a question, begin with "By a show of hands," then ask the question. Otherwise, your introduction could turn into a signal for the jabberers in the audience to transfer the attention away from you and onto themselves.

A reference to a current or historical event also works as an introduction. But until you tell the audience how this information affects them or why it excites you, the audience is not fully engaged. Without looking at your notes, show your audience what happened to you and why it made an impact on you.

Hook the listener in the first minute. How? I repeat: Tell us why you are passionate about the topic. What's so fascinating about the topic? Find something about it that the audience can identify with. Use the emotional response you had that ignited your interest in the first place.

If you touch the hearts of your listeners, their minds will follow. And don't forget your sense of humor. People will remember the joke or the story before they remember the exact information.

What is my statement of purpose?

In other words, what is your thesis? Declare to the audience in a simple sentence what you are going to tell them in the overall speech. Then enumerate. If you want to leave your audience with a better understanding of how to have a good job interview, your thesis statement could be something like this:

> Your resume gets you in the door, but your interview gets you the job. Today I will show you four winning interview tips.

Now your audience knows what to expect.

What two to five main points do I want to make?

What points will you make so that the faces in the audience will have "I'm interested" written all over them?

You need to support your thesis. Do so by focusing on the most interesting aspects of your subject.

The organization of your informative speech could be sequential—what happens or happened first, what happens second, what happens next. When you gave your demonstration speech, you used a sequential pattern. This is what you do first . . . second . . . third.

You also can choose to organize your points in a spatial pattern— this is what happens here or there and beyond.

If the title of my informative speech is "The Worlds of Star Wars," my main points for expansion and explanation could be:

1. Tatooine
2. Hoth
3. Dagobah
4. Alderaan

If your ideas don't fit the sequential or the spatial pattern, you can use what I call the topical pattern—in other words, the "what I find most important" pattern.

If my informative speech title is "Flu Protection 101," my main points for expansion and explanation could be:

1. Flu vaccination
2. Hygiene
3. Diet
4. Sleep

If my informative speech title is "Job Interview Almighty," my main points for expansion and explanation could be:

1. Research the company.
2. Analyze and prepare yourself.
3. Anticipate questions.
4. Prepare the day before.

Once you have your four points, express them using the same type of sentence for each. If I am informing my audience about "The Worlds of Star Wars," I would begin the sections with these four sentences:

1. Tatooine is a giant desert.
2. Hoth is a vast ice chunk.
3. Dagobah is a swamp.
4. Alderaan is Earth-like.

What examples, anecdotes, humor, statistics, quotations or other information will support my main points?

Research, research, research. Please note that I did not say Google, Google, Google.

I can Google any subject and read about it. What are you, as a speaker, going to show me about your topic, and how are you going to show me so you're not just spewing what I can find on Google?

I don't want to feel like I am in school and sitting through my ten-thousandth speech. I want to be educated. Remember, there's a big difference between going to school and getting an education.

As you gather supporting material, make sure the information is relevant to your thesis statement. If you are persuading your audience to see things the way you do, all your supporting information must prove your point of view.

Do not just say a study said something. If you cite a study, you must say who conducted the study and when, and then present the findings. Be sure the studies you cite are current. Information must be either timely or timeless.

If I am informing my audience about "The Worlds of Star Wars," I would flesh out each section (Tatooine, Hoth, Dagobah and Alderaan) by:

> Describing it for the audience.
> Explaining what happens there.
> Showing them why it is special to the story.

How can I entertain the audience?

Every speech you give is a speech to entertain. Whether your speech is a demonstration or is informative, persuasive or motivational—if it is not entertaining, good luck getting your audience to listen. Even a speech with the unlikely title "The Argyll and Sutherland Highlanders" can be interesting. A student in one of my classes proposed this title, and I hoped he would change his mind before his presentation. He did not.

From the moment my student uttered the word "Argyll," his voice showed his passion for the topic. As he delivered his introduction, his interest in sharing his enthusiasm was evident. His material was well-researched, he enumerated four highlights about his topic, and with the help of his stepdaughter, to whom he read a story every night, his voice was entertaining.

What could have felt like a trip to the dentist became a presentation that could be a pitch for the History Channel. And the speaker left me wanting to know more about a topic that only days before I had been dreading hearing anything about.

How can I summarize briefly what I said to make my audience remember my main points?

"In conclusion . . ."

"To wrap up . . ."

"What I would most like you to remember about our time together is . . ."

Take any of these three suggestions and fill in the rest. Review the main points and tie them to the thesis. And keep it brief!

How will I close my speech?

This is the punctuation at the end of your concluding summary. Do you have a final quotation you could use to end the speech? Another story?

My favorite way to close is to refer back to my opening story, quotation or statistic—a technique called book ending. If at the start of the speech you didn't give the ending, you can do that now. Or you can show how differently the story of an event you experienced would have been if you had known what you know now. Or you could show how you have changed because of the information you have shared in your speech.

A student whose speech was titled "The Cycle of Abuse" told of the negative effects abuse had had on her life and the lives of others. She remained objective throughout the speech and did not turn her presentation into a pity party. She closed her speech with this statement: "Abuse may be the reason you act this way, but don't let it become an excuse to stay this way."

Another student, whose topic was "A.D.D. Nation," told what A.D.D. is and how it has defined her, then closed her speech with a visual of history's most decorated Olympian, swimmer Michael Phelps. The final words of her speech: "Don't make your diagnosis your excuse. He didn't."

Giving a Successful Informative Speech

- Outline your topic. If you must write a narrative first, you still will need to outline because only an outline should accompany you to the podium.

- Make sure that your speech clearly supports your thesis statement. Know your purpose and stick to it.

- Practice your speech. You've heard this before, but let me repeat my advice for emphasis: Practice your speech—*out loud*. You do not present your speech in your head, so practice audibly, *aloud*, out loud! You are, in essence, test marketing your presentation.

- Respect the occasion by wearing appropriate clothing when you are presenting.

- If you're informing us about thrash metal or any kind of music you may love, have samples of the music.

- If Alvin Ailey is your favorite dance company, show photos and a few short choreography clips that help your audience see why.

- If your topic is how to write a resume, show us with a handout that supports your presentation. Give me something tangible that I can take home.

- If you quote someone, you must credit that someone.

- If you have a statistic, credit the organization that compiled the statistic.

FYI: Know Your Sources

After one presenter gave several startling statistics to open her speech, I asked her for the source from which the statistics were gathered. "Off the Internet," she said.

The Internet!

What does that mean? The Internet is not an organized storehouse of information like a library. It is simply a collection of interconnected networks (thus "inter-net"), which allows millions of computers to communicate with each other using internationally standardized protocols. Sounds like technical mumbo jumbo. For most people it probably is, but the important point is that this accurate description of the Internet contains no reference to where the information comes from or how real it is.

That's because the Internet per se is not a source but just something that organizes websites that *say* they are sources.

For most people, getting information from the Internet means asking a search engine like Google or Yahoo to find references to the topic they are searching for. Next, from the many thousands of references returned, they choose one that seems to best supply the specific information they seek.

What's missing? In terms of real information, almost everything.

I have never studied the herding instincts of Tibetan terriers, nor have I ever even seen one. However, for only a few dollars a month, I could use the website name www.TibetanTerrierExperts.com and publish authoritative-sounding articles on this topic. Few people will question my word, and it is nearly certain that one of these articles or the website name will show up as a referenced source in some college presentation. That is the big problem with the Internet as a substitute for a library. It is very difficult to trace the authenticity of the information. You must know the source.

When researching, use more than the Internet. Go to the library.

Exercise #12
The Informative Speech

Make your presentation—in front of the class, or if you are going this alone, on Skype or video. Don't *tell* your class or Skype audience. *Show* your interest in and knowledge of the topic you chose.

Why? Because your knowledge is important and can be helpful to others. Share it.

_____

Informative Speech Checklist

Once you've given your informative speech, answer these questions about yourself from the audience's perspective. Remember, the person in question is you. And the checklist below is not about positive feedback, it's about telling the truth.

For each question, respond with a *yes* if the presenter is at least 70 percent competent or with a *no* if the presenter is less than 70 percent competent.

1. Does this person command your attention with a strong beginning?

2. Are you curious to know more about the speaker and what he or she has to say?

3. Is the speaker's purpose clear to the audience?

4. Does the speaker develop unified support for the thesis that includes examples, details and evidence?

5. Has the speaker organized the presentation coherently to support the thesis?

6. Does the speaker incorporate appropriate information from research material to support the thesis, and does he cite it correctly?

7. Does the speaker appear gracious and friendly to the audience?

8. Does the speaker use sentences that are grammatically sound?

9. Does the speaker enunciate and project?

10. Can you follow what the speaker is saying?

Exercise #13
Review the Index Card Almighty

In Exercise #10, following your demonstration speech, you wrote down three things you did well. Take a look at your Index Card Almighty. Did you do just as well in your informative speech?

Then there were those three things that needed improvement. Well?

After you look at the index card, review the Informative Speech Checklist provided above to evaluate yourself from the audience's perspective.

Why? If all your answers are *yes*, you win a trip to Hawaii! (Just kidding, but isn't it nice to get a high score?)

_____

Chapter Four:
It Isn't Just Words

Using Body Language to Show without Telling

In the movie *Hitch*, Will Smith plays a professional dating doctor who treats heartsick schlubs. In the opening scene, he gives this advice.

HITCH

> Sixty percent of all human communication is nonverbal body language. Thirty percent is your tone. So that means that ninety percent of what you're saying ain't coming out of your mouth.

Isn't it amazing that ninety percent of communication is rarely taught in our educational system? It is barely mentioned. Many people feel they are ignorant on the subject when it's the primary and most honest way that we communicate.

We learn body language before we learn spoken language. A two-year-old child can interpret a glance from his mother across the room and respond to it. The glance can say, "Sit down," "Shut up," "I love you," "I am proud of you" or a hundred other commands or statements. We were dependent upon body language to communicate before we learned language.

The problem with body language is not our understanding of it. The problem is that we fail to take responsibility for what we say (sometimes even scream) with our bodies. Subtle body movements send loud messages, and the accuracy of these body movements far outweighs the verbal accompaniment.

Let's put your command of your body language to the test in the next exercise—a variant on a game you have most likely played in the past.

Exercise #14
Nuked Charades

Everyone close your book, except for one person. If you are that person or if you are using this book on your own (in which case you will also need to assemble a small group of friends), go to the back of the book and copy, cut out or scroll through the "Nuked Charades" pages in Appendix B.

Each person playing gets one category, but only when it's his turn. If you run out of categories, make up your own.

Round One: State your category to the class or to your friends. Then you have one minute to describe the 10 words in the category. When someone guesses the word you're describing, move to the next word.

Round Two: State your category, then do the same as the above, but this time *nonverbally!*

Why? To get more than your mouth moving.

Your mood, movement and manner speak reams before you even open your mouth. They can help empower and express your sense of self-worth or diminish your confidence and feed your insecurity. So what are you saying before you open your mouth?

Your clothes frame your body language. Fair or not, people make assumptions based on the way you dress. When you give a presentation, you must hit a balance between stiffly dressed up and so casual that you do not seem to respect the occasion.

I am not going to ask you to take a sobering look in the mirror. Instead, I'd like you to look back at your informative speech. What did you wear when you presented? Was it consistent with the message you wanted to express?

I'll help you decide whether or not it was appropriate by giving you another question.

But first think about this: We all want to feel comfortable in what we wear. We want to express ourselves, stand out, blend in, be part of the fashion scene—but it's not about us when we are giving a speech. It's about the audience.

Here's the question:

> Is your audience listening to you or looking at your clothes, hair and accoutrements—your piercings, tattoos, hats, makeup, branding, jewelry, nails or hair?

One student gave a demonstration speech on how to administer C.P.R. She wore low-cut jeans, and every time she bent over to demonstrate mouth-to-mouth resuscitation, the audience had a clear view of the large tattoo on the small of her back. Although the guys in the class liked the speech, it was not for the presenter's public speaking skills, but for that body art. I suspect they heard little of the information presented.

When giving a speech, women and men alike should wear something that would be appropriate for a managerial-level job interview. Or imagine you are dining at a fancy restaurant and meeting your future in-laws for the first time. Or what if you were to go before a judge—what would you wear? For all of these occasions, you must show respect and a professional style. No jeans, no shoes you could wear on a playground, no cleavage, no ink.

Gentleman: Wear a button-down shirt, but a tie is optional. Tuck your shirt in, and keep in mind that no one wants to see your underwear while you are standing or sitting. Wear a belt. Don't tell me you don't have money for dress pants. Check out sale racks or thrift stores, where you should find a pair of pants for around $10. Jeans are not dress pants. If you need a shave, shave. If you have a beard, trim it so it doesn't look like you've been on a ten-day hunting trip. Finally, no caps—ever—in an interview or when you're giving a presentation.

Ladies: Black pants or a skirt and a plain blouse work. I would opt for the skirt instead of pants. But wear a skirt only if it is no more than two inches above the knee and you have a nice pair of matching heels. Practice walking in those heels. You don't want to look like an ostrich as you walk to the podium or into the interview. No sandals or jeans.

If the topic of your speech suggests special garb, you can dress in a costume or ethnic clothing. If your presentation is about your favorite team in the NFL, then it's appropriate to ditch the button-down shirt for a jersey. If you are demonstrating the proper gear for jumping out of an airplane, then ditch the skirt.

Exercise #15
Go Shopping

Look into your closet. If you see only jeans, T-shirts and athletic shoes, you need to go shopping. The thrift store or the sale rack will have all you need, for cheap, as will stores like Old Navy and H&M.

Why? Because it's important to show you care. And it isn't just your words that communicate that.

Posture

I am so thankful for the years of dance training I had because it gave me posture that says I am confident. That's what your posture should say—and it does when you stand up straight. That means the head is in line with the shoulders, and the shoulders are directly over the hips.

If your head juts beyond your shoulders, you look like a chicken. If your shoulders jut ahead of your hips, it looks like you're trying to overcompensate for a small chest. If your hips jut forward, you look like you're on a fashion show runway.

Go back to the last time you were feeling great about yourself. Realize how you walked when you felt great. Then go back to the last time you had bad feelings about yourself. Realize how you walked when you had those negative feelings.

Our posture—behind the podium or when we walk—signals to the world how we feel about ourselves and about the world.

When our head is down and we shuffle along, we signal laziness and bad feelings. When our head is up and we step out in determined, purposeful strides, we signal energy and good feelings.

What are you watching? Instead: Whom are you watching?

Although I've mentioned this a couple of times earlier, I'm going to repeat it for emphasis: Public speaking is not public reading. Eye contact is imperative if you want to establish communication with your audience. If you don't want to establish communication with them, hand them your notes and tell them what to Google.

Notes that you read word for word are a poor substitute for preparation and rehearsal. The topic you present is not just about information. It's about your take on the information.

When you speak, your eyes involve your listeners; they convey that you are sincere and interested, and they show that you care about whether your audience accepts the message. No matter how large your audience may be, each listener wants to feel that you are talking to him or her on a personal level.

Yes, it's fine to refer to your notes and read during a presentation if there is a quotation, statistic, study finding or fully developed plan that needs to be delivered verbatim. In these cases the use of projected PowerPoint slides can facilitate your delivery.

Notes are also your safety net in case your mind goes blank. But make sure you know the content well enough that you can lift up your eyes and focus them back onto your audience after just a short time.

Even if you never give another speech after you read this book, you're likely to attend many meetings throughout your life.

Whether in a meeting or when giving a speech, the need for eye contact remains. Why?

Meetings always have a specific purpose, and it is important to know who is or is not paying attention. It is also wise to watch for someone who might be questioning, not understanding or possibly disagreeing with your message. For all of these eventualities, direct eye contact with listeners will allow you to provide immediate and accurate feedback.

When questions arise, maintaining eye contact with the questioner shows that you are focused on what that person is asking. It also has a side benefit—it signals to others not to interrupt while you are engaged with the current question.

Sometimes a message you are delivering may be a bit hard to take. There will be those who disagree or who could not care less. Maintaining eye contact with an audience is a signal to them that you are committed to your subject.

Triangle Your Audience

If you can do so, move away from the podium occasionally as you talk, which is preferable to remaining glued in one spot. Move stage left, then stage right, then go back to the center. Repeat a few times during the course of the speech. If your venue requires that you stay at the podium, divide the audience into three sections. Look at individuals within each section as you deliver your speech.

What does this have to do with body language? When you are with friends and someone is talking but you are excluded from any eye contact, don't you begin to wonder if you are invisible? The same goes for an audience. Even if you remain behind the podium, you still need to look at all the triangles of your audience.

Gesture

I know a speech professor who will not give a lecture if anyone in the class sits with crossed arms. That gesture signals that the student is closed off to learning and discussion. (This professor teaches in southern California. If you're in a cold classroom in New England, however, crossed arms may be a necessity for survival!)

Wherever you are as a presenter, don't parade around the room with your arms crossed for long. Crossed arms translate as closed off and arrogant.

The next time you're sitting next to someone on a couch, notice the position of his or her legs—whether they are positioned toward you or away. This is a signal about whether he or she wants to get to know you better. Legs positioned toward you means the person is interested in knowing you better. If they're positioned away from you, probably not.

A speaker who uses open-palmed gestures signals that he is open and approachable. A speaker who holds her hands tightly behind her back is not.

As a speaker, be aware that your audience is also telling you something with their body language:

- An audience that is fidgeting or looking around is bored.
- Listeners with wrinkled brows are puzzled or contemplating.
- People wringing their hands or clicking pens are anxious or nervous.
- Those who shrug their shoulders are experiencing indifference.
- Gritting teeth signify anger.
- Rolling eyes reveal skepticism or disgust.

- A mouth that drops open expresses disbelief.
- When a hand covers the mouth, the person is surprised or shocked.
- Someone who bites his lip is usually concentrating or thinking.
- A person who looks off into the distance is feeling indifferent or is daydreaming.

True or False: Just be yourself.

False! As long as you don't project nervousness, doubt, disbelief, boredom or nonchalance, then yes, just be yourself. Otherwise, show confidence, authority and credibility, even if this means you have to pretend for the first few minutes of your speech. To get started "on the right foot" . . .

- Stand straight—a position of power.
- Focus on the audience as a group of friends in need of the knowledge you are about to give them.
- Hold on to the podium as you begin your presentation.

As you get into the speech, practice moving away from the podium—movement makes you much more engaging. The podium can easily turn into a security blanket. If you need to be miked, then yes, you will need to stay at the podium, unless you have a body mike.

However, don't pace in front of your audience. Move for a reason. Pacing is interpreted as a nervous behavior; people read it as a sign of insecurity.

Faking It

No, I don't want you to just be yourself and make the audience uncomfortable when you are nearly choking with nervousness.

And yes, there are dead giveaways that let an audience see right through you if you are faking it.

People can detect from a speaker's body language if he or she has not done the research, not studied the notes and not practiced out loud. Those clues include:

- Excessive face touching, such as scratching the nose, touching the forehead or holding the hand up to the mouth for a cough that didn't exist before the speech began.
- A lot of blinking and a lack of eye contact with the audience; gazing into the air as if searching for clues on what to say next.
- A stiff expression in which few facial muscles are used; the result is a creepy smile, and sometimes nervous speakers don't even attempt a smile.
- Folded arms or an object—for example, a container of coffee—placed between the speaker and the audience.
- A very fast pace, signaling that any silence makes the presenter feel uncomfortable. The faster the speaker speaks, the less the audience thinks.
- A speaker who talks in circles, never getting to the point; this kind of presentation is usually impossible to follow.
- A speaker who avoids the use of contractions, which results in speech that sounds unnatural (though sometimes the full treatment—*I cannot* rather than *I can't*—is a useful tool for strongly making a point).

Facial Expression

If you focus on your notes and not on the audience, your listeners will not see any of your facial expressions. Instead, focus on your audience, and use facial expressions that communicate an emotional connection to the material you are presenting.

People in the audience want to know how your material has affected you. As you speak, are you boasting, challenging, convincing, educating, enlightening, joking, mocking, provoking, questioning, remembering, solving, warning. We need to be able to read your intention and the emotion in your face.

We have all had that teacher who just stands at the chalkboard or sits behind his desk, regurgitating dry information from a textbook that even he finds uninteresting. He doesn't deserve the tribute, so don't emulate him.

A word of warning: If you cannot remain objective during your presentation and your facial expression turns to tears, you are too emotionally involved with your topic. I like this analogy: If you are describing a swimming pool, you should not be splashing around in the middle of it. You need to swim to the side of the pool, get out of the pool, and then observe and describe it.

If your face says negative, you will be perceived as negative. If your face says positive, guess what? You look and sound like a different person. Facial expression often mirrors tone.

Tone

The voice, in addition to speaking words, expresses feelings and attitudes that are conveyed by the way we say words. That's *tone*. The words we speak carry the information we wish to convey, but our attitude about that information is carried by both our body language and the way we color our words.

Thankfully, most of us have been taught from a very early age to say *please* and *thank you*. It's too bad that what few of us were taught is how to say these words in the right tone at the right time. *Please* and *thank you* can be said many different ways that convey many different meanings—like *please* for "I'm desperate" or *thank you* for "I hate you." It's all in the tone. Ask someone how they are and see the hundreds of meanings *I'm fine* can send.

Some people use the same tone for every word, and people who listen to them have an experience similar to staring at a monochrome painting.

A great acting exercise is to take a line of dialogue and expand it with your own words. Actors do this to help them get to the meaning of the words the playwright or screenwriter has written.

Let's take a look at the beginning of Jeremy's unprepared speech, below. First, see what he said, and then see how I use the acting exercise to show what he was really saying as he read from his notes.

What he said: "Hello, my name is Jeremy Hudson and I'm goin' to talk to you about thrasher metal. My speech is on this because ever since I was a kid, whenever I went to my uncle's, he'd be playing it. Gotta say it used to scare me."

What he said (in boldface) and what he conveyed (in italics):

> **Hello, my name is Jeremy Hudson** *I think that's my name 'cause my tone just went up at the last syllable of my name, turning it into a question, and I really don't want to be up here, as you can hear by my lack of volume and my eyes looking down* **and I'm goin' to talk to you about thrasher metal.** *Might as well turn my subject into a question also. And, like, I didn't read or listen to how I should start a speech, so I'm just wingin' it, and if I would take the time to form my words I might say going instead of goin'.* **My speech is on this because ever since I was a kid, whenever I went to my uncle's, he'd be playing it.** *So, had I read this book, Show, Don't Tell, I would know to just get into the story about goin' to my uncle's house.* **Gotta**

say it used to scare me. *I didn't think that maybe since I'm talkin about music, like, maybe I should play some.*

Pronunciation & Articulation

Poor articulation says, *I'm too lazy to form my words.* The audience's reaction is *You're not credible.* Lazy mouth also makes your audience strain to understand you. On the flip side, any hint of *I'm better than you are* can go over badly.

You don't need to speak English perfectly, but you do need to have a respect for the language you're speaking in class. Learn to pronounce words according to what the dictionary shows.

Some common mispronunciations are:

> *axe* for *ask*
> *congradulations* for *congratulations*
> *crick* for *creek*
> *don't cha* for *don't you*
> *draw* for *drawer*
> *droppin'* for *dropping*, for example (*droppin'* the *ing* and only *sayin'* an *in* instead of an *ing*)
> *edgeacation* for *education*
> *emporend* for *important*
> *Feberry* for *February*
> *framiliar* for *familiar*
> *git* for *get*
> *goverment* for *government*
> *INsurance* for *inSURance*
> *jew* for *you*
> *liberry* for *library*
> *pitcher* for *picture*
> *recanize* for *recognize*
> *ruff* for *roof*
> *suprise* for *surprise*

t's and *d*'s that are dropped at the end of a word
wha for *what*

You cannot practice these a few hours before your presentation. You must use them as part of your everyday speech.

Projection

When I ask a question and I hear *I dah nah* for *I don't know*, it's clear to me that this person's words are formed in the back of the throat, not in the mouth. One needs to use one's mouth to project.

But projection does not mean shouting. Generally, if you articulate your words, if you speak purposefully and if you are focused on your message, you will project.

If you could see your words coming out of your mouth, you would want them to flow forward, not drop out of your mouth and hit the floor. This principle holds true even when you are miked. Microphones may amplify sound, but they also highlight lisps, mumbles and drawls.

Exercise #16
Pronunciation & Tone

Open your mouth and punctuate the endings of words so that everyone in the back of the class can hear you. Speak slowly enough that your mouth has time to form the words, not regurgitate them. Remember to fully pronounce that *d*.

> How much wood would a woodchuck chuck,
> If a woodchuck could chuck wood?
> He'd chuck as much wood as a woodchuck could,
> If a woodchuck could chuck wood.
> How much wood would a woodchuck chuck,
> If a woodchuck could chuck wood?
> A woodchuck would chuck all the wood he could chuck,
> If a woodchuck would chuck wood.

Let's add tone to this verbal workout by preparing an effective reading of the poem on the next page.

In preparation, think about coloring your words so that you paint a picture for your audience. Is that picture bright or dark? Give the audience the time to experience the thought and feeling that drive the words.

Do you tend to say every word in the same tone? Is there little variance in the sound you produce? Are any of your vocal effects labored or forced? *No* can be a beautiful word. With these considerations in mind, share this poem out loud.

> Walk bravely through the darkness.
> The stillness of the night wraps about us.
> A cool breeze whispers through the trees.
> Walking along the mile-long road,
> Around the bend the road continues.

Now quicken the pace with hope of warmth.
The cold grows more intense.
Suddenly there is a hint of light,
Then a thin ribbon on the horizon.
Ever so slowly the ribbon widens,
First of russet, then a show of purest gold.
Resting on the horizon through a slit peers the sun.
Slowly it rises, we feel its warmth.
Dawn is breaking.
A new day is here.

Why? No one wants to hear boring. Wake up your voice!

That All-Important 10 Percent That Does Come Out of Your Mouth

We should all be tweaking our vocabulary as we go through life. There are plenty of mobile-device apps that can easily help with this. I downloaded the Official SAT Question of the Day app. It also challenges my grammatical skills.

Most words have at least three definitions. According to *The Random House College Dictionary*, the word *love* has twenty-two nuances and variations in usage. *Lose* has twenty-four. So choose your words with care. The various people who will hear them may react differently to the same word. Know your audience, for they will be influenced by your word choice—for better or for worse.

Stay away from unusual words. A former boss told me I was perspicuous. I had no idea whether I had just received a compliment or a put-down. When I Googled the meaning, I laughed at the irony. He used a word that means easy to understand. Really? Who understands *perspicuous* except a handful of lexicographers (an author or editor of a dictionary)?

My point is that bloated words cloud and confuse. You need to keep your vocabulary in tune with those you are speaking to. If you must use an unusual word, define it for your listeners.

Watch your grammar. Nothing discredits a speaker more quickly than using the incorrect form for a verb. In closing a speech, a student of mine said, "The United States should have never went to war." That is all I remember of his ten-minute speech. We've got the present: *go*. We've got the past: *went*. We've got the past perfect (when you add a *have, has* or *had* to the equation): *gone*.

Review the list of irregular verbs given in Appendix A. No, don't review them, memorize them!

In general, avoid abbreviations. If you are speaking at work, you can assume that people will know the abbreviations for technical terms. But if you are giving instructions in a speech to a friend or to your classmates, you can assume nothing. "You can't connect my computer directly to the TV, because my computer only has SVGA and DivX outputs, but the TV needs HDMI. So you can either use SVGA with an RGB connection to the TV or you can use a DivX to HDMI adapter cable" is Greek to me.

Never, ever, ever use swear words. Ever.

Avoid filler words that mean nothing. *Yadda-yadda-yadda* is on the top of my list. *Basically* is a close second. *Basically* is basically a basic time filler for people who basically can't get to the point, basically. *So on and so forth, you know, blah-blah-blah, anyways, like, a lot, uh* and *um* are all verbal farts. And please don't end any sentence with *ya know what I'm sayin?*

It's fine to deviate from political correctness. As Larry King said, "Let's not become so worried about not offending anybody that we lose the ability to distinguish between respect and paranoia."

Rehearsal: To Be Proud, Say It Aloud

You've chosen a topic, gathered information and written your outline. At last the real work begins. Completion of these first steps can make your rehearsal more efficient, but to be proud, say it aloud.

Rehearse your speech at least three times, preferably in front of an audience, even if that audience is your pet. Rehearsal gives you focus.

When you are writing and researching your speech, words form in your head differently than how they actually sound. When you are speaking out loud, you will hear when your speech stumbles. You'll know when you've gone on for too long with your points. You're more likely to hear grammatical mistakes.

Saying your speech helps you formulate a better second draft, something even professional speech writers routinely do.

A Recap of Essentials

Use self-start techniques by doing one or more of the following:

- Pretend you are looking at a person you would like to meet (a celebrity or a desired mentor).
- Imagine that you are the expert on a topic and you have come to the rescue in a tough situation.
- Pretend that something wonderful has just happened to you (you've landed the job of your dreams).
- Believe that what you are doing is important.

Think about how you will introduce your topic:

- Hear a question (in your head) about your topic.
- The first line of your speech should be in response to that question.
- Make visual contact with your audience.

Set your posture, eye contact and volume, and always project:

- Do not hunch. Stand up straight.
- Focus on your audience with sustained eye contact. If you turn your back to the audience to look at a visual, your volume must increase. Assume you are speaking to someone who is slightly hard of hearing (I said *slightly*).
- Open your mouth vertically and project your words as if you can see them floating straight forward, not dropping to the ground as they fall out of your mouth.

Practice, practice, practice:

- Do not blow off the advice given above.
- Prepare your speech in outline form or using the template of your choice.
- Practice out loud! Don't do it in front of a mirror, because you are not giving the speech to yourself. For this first rehearsal, being alone in a car is good. Then move on and give your speech to a person.
- Become better through effort; avoid excuses.

Dress for the occasion:

- Choose something you would wear to a job interview for a six-figure salary.
- Don't wear an outfit that's too colorful or has too many prints.
- Do wear something that conceals tattoos.

If you blow it:

- Ask if you can begin again.
- Crack a joke about your dilemma, but just one.

But if you implement the suggestions presented in this chapter, your chances of blowing it will decrease dramatically.

Chapter Five:
Ready, Set, Sell

Potent Tactics to Sell Your Ideas

In public speaking, the essential goal is to always strive for clear communication. Roadblocks on the road to clear communication include expressing yourself via the lingo of texting, using language heard only in the region where you live ("wicked awesome") and speaking like Jeff Dunham, the ventriloquist, without the dummies.

Getting Ready

Relying on the basics is what gets you ready. Every athlete, no matter what her level of accomplishment, begins every day with the essentials. Even as a professional, she does the same exercises she did when she was an amateur. The same exercises, day after day.

I've said it before, but I'll repeat: The finest speech can be ruined by mumbling, dropping word endings and slurring syllables. Do you have to repeat what you say to your listeners? If people can't understand you the first time you say something, don't blame their hearing. More likely, the error lies in the way you said it.

Reading out loud is excellent practice. Reading to children is as good as it gets because you will instantly know if you are holding their interest. Unless you pronounce the words of a story distinctly and with a touch of drama, most kids will be jumping around the room by the time the fairy godmother makes her appearance.

So let's warm up the facial and imaginative muscles that, when you use them, add expression to your face, clarity to your words and enthusiasm for your topic.

Exercise #17
Macbeth, Act 1, Scene 7

Shakespeare?! That's probably your first question. Here are others I've heard from students:

*Why do I have to say this ****?* You're doing it to open your mouth vertically, to practice forming word endings and to learn to tap in to the emotion of the character.

What does this speech even mean? Macbeth is thinking about killing King Duncan and the consequences he will face if he does so. He wishes we weren't held accountable for our actions, and he fears the destruction that unchecked ambition can bring to the individual and to society.

How do I do this? This character is frustrated, fearful and angry, but he's trying to stay in control. Enunciate the words in the following passages as if it were very important that your voice be heard.

But I'm never going to talk like Shakespeare! Maybe not. But this exercise in reading his words will help you:

- Improve your voice.
- Slow down, which in turn will calm you down.
- Make a connection with the audience on an emotional level even though you feel like you're speaking Greek.

Remember, you are to speak the words out loud. (I've reformatted the speech to make it easier for you to enunciate the words.)

If it were done
when 'tis done,
then 'twere well
it were done quickly.
If the assassination
could trammel up the consequence,
and catch with his surcease
success;
that but this blow
might be the be-all and the end-all here,
but here,
upon this bank and shoal of time,
we'd jump the life to come.
But in these cases
we still have judgment here;
that we but teach
bloody instructions,
which, being taught,
return to plague the inventor.
This even-handed justice
commends the ingredients
of our poison'd chalice
to our own lips.

———————————————————

Getting Set

If you're a runner, getting set means stepping into the starting blocks.

If you're a speaker, getting set means doing another exercise. Practice isn't easy, but it makes a face plant less likely in the long run.

Our next speech is the persuasive speech. The goal is to make your audience think the way you do. To accomplish this, chose words that will encourage shared meaning, evoke an emotional response and spur the listener to action.

Exercise #18
Making Your Audience Think Like You

With no feedback from the audience, get busy, take turns and convince your audience in one minute to . . .

> Let you borrow $100.
> Leave the classroom.
> Buy your car (if you don't have one, even better).
> Never text again.
> Do your homework.
> Vote for you.
> Stop whining.

Or convince your audience that . . .

> You are the best-dressed person in the room.
> Your ex-boyfriend is an alien from outer space.
> You have been nominated for an Academy Award.
> We have all won a trip to Hawaii.
> You have fallen and broken your leg.

Why? This exercise is an excellent way to get ready to sell an idea. It is also a pathway to further explore expressing yourself with increased ease and accuracy.

———————————————

The Pitch

No, I'm not talking about the singsongy speech patterns some people play like a personal theme song whenever they speak. I'm talking about something we all learned how to do very early on, probably at Toys "R" Us.

Remember that toy you really, really, really wanted? That toy your parents said you couldn't have? If you walked out of the store with toy in hand, chances are it was not because of the tantrum you threw but because of the words you used.

Life's a pitch.

You pitch to your parents when you need a loan. If you're a salesperson, you pitch to prospective clients. If you have an invention, you pitch to potential investors. If you've gone to a college fair, the guy at the booth pitched to you. If you go to a job fair, you pitch to the gal at the booth. Taking an idea to someone with the power to do something about it is a pitch.

That someone is asking the question *What is it you want me to do?* Answer that and you're golden. If you can't, you don't get the money, you don't sell the product, you'd better not be really interested in that college, you don't get the job.

The short, focused pitch is commonly called an *elevator pitch* because it can be delivered in the brief time one is in an elevator—perhaps a rare moment when a key manager or executive is your captive audience—and it covers the key message:

- What is your product or service?
- What is its value to the customer?
- Why is it the best thing out there?

A pitch sums your idea or what you're selling in a way that leaves your audience saying *yes*.

Shark Tank is a long-running reality show on which successful business people listen to and rip apart hopeful start-up entrepreneurs. According to Barbara Corcoran, one of the show's judges, "My most important criteria when making the decision to invest are (1) do I trust the individual and (2) do they have the fire in their belly to bring the business to the finish line?" This is what you must accomplish with your pitch.

Like any other skill, pitching takes practice. Let's begin with an everyday pitch that is simple, but useful: You are going to convince your friends to watch the movie you want to see. If you've done that, then you've pitched.

If you haven't, get ready, get set . . .

Let's *sell*.

This time we'll start with an exercise.

Exercise #19
Movie Pitch, Elevator-Style

Choose your favorite movie. Sure, you may have several, but which one have you watched over and over and over.

Think about why you like this movie and why others will enjoy it too. What is your reason? Make sure you answer that question.

Give a one-minute pitch of that movie. Include a brief plot summary and state the reason you know your friends will like it too and should watch it. Remember, you have just one minute to deliver your pitch.

Why? We live in a sound-bite society. Learning to get your thoughts across succinctly—being able to convince someone quickly that what you want or what you have is valuable—is a game changer.

Another way to learn how to sell an idea is to turn on the television or go online and watch commercials. Commercials show us why the viewer should think a certain way—a way that leads to buying a product or agreeing with an idea. Every commercial is a bite-size persuasive speech.

Commercials are excellent examples of how to deliver a speech. Every word in a commercial should say "I want to help you." When a commercial is delivered well, the actor makes a connection with the audience and creates a sense of aliveness.

The customers watching it see the actor, hear her voice and think, *She seems like a nice person, someone I can relate to. I'd like to hear what she has to say.*

With a persuasive speech, the name of the game is *to sell*. A winning strategy motivates the listener to act by using the power of persuasion. You can unlock the power of a persuasive speech by using a template called Monroe's Motivated Sequence.

Monroe's Motivated Sequence

This template, developed by Professor Alan Monroe at Purdue University and implemented by the advertising industry since the 1930s, quickly leads the listener on a path to a desired action. It screams, "Do something!" That something could be to buy a product or an idea, donate time or money, recycle, vote for me, pass a law.

This method is used because it still works. It can also be used to organize presentations that will deliver results.

Throw a stick at a television commercial and you'll probably hit Monroe's Motivated Sequence. The sequence has five steps that address the psychology of persuasion.

Step One—Attention

The beginning of a commercial grabs the listener's attention. It relates the message to the audience and shows the importance of the topic by evoking curiosity: with a question, a tale, a picture or a startling statement.

The attention part of the commercial answers the question

Why should I listen?

Let's look at a cold medication ad:

A woman is breathing but holding her hand to her nose in obvious pain.

Step Two—Need

This section demonstrates that there is a problem that directly affects the viewer. It shows why there is a problem with the existing situation. It can back up an image with statistics, examples or testimony. By the end of this step, listeners should be so concerned about the problem that they are primed to hear your solution.

The need part of the commercial answers the question

Why do I need to know?

Let's continue with the cold medication ad:

Winter is coming, and so is nasal congestion.

Step Three—Satisfaction

The midpoint of the commercial shows listeners how to satisfy the need. It presents the plan for a solution—the product. It gives the audience a clear understanding of how the product will work.

The satisfaction part of the commercial answers the question

How can I do something?

Now it's time for the all-important visual of the cold medication:

Tavid-D

Step Four—Visualization

This part of the commercial shows what life will be like with the need satisfied. The audience sees how much better conditions become once a particular solution is brought to bear. Strong visuals and strong imagery are key.

The visualization part of the commercial answers the question

How would something be different or improved?

Feel the effects of this cold medication:

The woman is shown once again, this time breathing easily.

Step Five—Action

The ending urges listeners to do something about the problem—
now. It says exactly what your audience should do and how to do
it. A final appeal reinforces the necessity to act.

The action part of the commercial answers the question

> *What is it I can do?*

The finale of the cold medication ad:

Recall the earlier pain, show the product again,
then present the woman, with her happiness
restored.

Following these five steps allows you to shape an effective
presentation. Monroe's Motivated Sequence will empower you to
provide a more efficient and effective view of your product or
idea.

Spend some time looking at a few of your favorite commercials
online. See how they follow Monroe's Motivated Sequence. After
you do, you'll be ready to tackle the next exercise.

Exercise #20
Show Me à la M.M.S.

YouTube your favorite commercial and break down the segments into Monroe's Motivated Sequence.

My favorite is the Snickers "diva commercial."

Attention: As the commercial opens, we see a lone car traveling down a long and winding road. How symbolic of life. It's something we can all relate to. Add someone in the back seat complaining in your ear, especially a diva like Aretha Franklin, and you've got a bad trip.

Need: When a fellow traveler attempts comfort, Aretha slaps him. This is going to be a miserable trip unless something is done about a slapping diva. She could cause bodily harm!

Satisfaction: Thank goodness, someone suggests a Snickers bar to save the day and transform that diva back into the pleasant friend he really is.

Visualization: The diva takes a bite of a Snickers bar and, violà, the diva turns into the friend.

Action: Uh-oh! Another diva appears in the front seat. This time the complainer is Liza Minnelli. A voice says, "You're not you when you're hungry." A Snickers bar fills the screen, and the voice continues: "Snickers satisfies." The mighty voice tells us exactly what we need to do and how to do it. Eat that Snickers.

Show your class or yourself how your favorite commercial follows the M.M.S.

Why? You'll see how easy it is to be persuasive the same way the pros do it, using an easily applicable formula—Monroe's Motivated Sequence.

Being Persuasive

In the persuasive speech, your product might be a controversial topic that oozes with problems. Or it could be an agreeable topic that your audience just hasn't done anything about, like "Don't Text and Drive." You take that topic and try to open minds to your way of thinking. It is the perfect platform to allow your voice to be heard.

Once you lift their eyelids, you have a chance to get people moving. Getting people to listen to you requires that you be nice. Be considerate. Be helpful. Be upbeat. Show your audience how they will benefit—how listening to you will be worth their time. If you don't, you are the equivalent of a bad commercial, and your audience will get up and stare into the refrigerator, in search of something more tantalizing.

The following outline shows how one speaker used Monroe's Motivated Sequence in a speech urging classmates to stop eating meat.

When you begin to fill in your template, think

>*I want to leave my audience with a better understanding of . . .*

In this case, the topic is why it is important to stop eating meat.

The title of this speech could be—again, for the purpose of focusing on a topic and creating an outline for your speech— "Meat Madness."

Attention: Imagine a series of pictures: several hundred cattle bunched together waiting for slaughter; live chickens hung by their feet over a conveyor belt; hundreds of pigs jammed into pens. Yes, a picture is worth a thousand words. The presenter said, "This is the before," as the audience viewed each picture. She then held up a McDonald's hamburger, a bucket of Kentucky Fried Chicken and a rack of ribs and said, "This is the after. This meat is loaded with hormones, drugs, fat and cruelty."

Need: She explained how these methods of raising and slaughtering animals affect our health and our wallets. "Eating meat not only inflicts severe cruelty on the animals to be slaughtered but poses a threat to our health with the diseases and health hazards carried to us from these animals." She showed bullet points with statistics to highlight her thesis; for example, according to the U.S. Department of Agriculture, in 2011 more than 10 million animals that were diseased when they were slaughtered were still processed for human consumption.

Satisfaction: She showed pictures of animals from local farms, where they were not in pens, subjected to filth or pumped with hormones. She pointed out that cruelty to animals and the threats to our environment and our health could be solved by a decision to stop eating meat that comes from "factory farms." "This afternoon, I would like to share with you three alternatives to lessen or eliminate meat consumption. First, for those who find that prospect incomprehensible, start purchasing meat from local farms."

Visualization: There's a common perception that removing meat from the menu is dangerous because it will mean a loss of protein in our diets. So the speaker also showed pictures of protein-rich foods that can be substituted for meat. "My second suggestion is based on the fact that beans, potatoes, wheat, rice, broccoli, spinach, almonds, peas, peanut butter, tofu, soymilk, lentils and kale—eaten as part of a varied diet and in the proper combinations—are excellent substitutes for meat." She showed visuals of these foods that contain the same or better nutritional values as those we get from meat. "We would all immediately feel the level of suffering on earth drop considerably at the same time we lose weight and avoid diseases that are carried by animals."

Action: Again she showed pictures of stockyards of cattle, conveyor belts of chickens and pens of pigs. She then showed a vegetarian burrito from Chipotle and a salad with bread from Panera. "This is the third alternative to meat consumption. If we all work together and drive past those fast-food joints that support animal cruelty, we will cut down on that cruelty, weight and disease, and will enjoy a healthier lifestyle."

All of the above statements would be of little value without support. Each statement and picture was backed with support— with examples, testimony, studies and magazine articles.

Now, you are ready, set and . . .

On the Road to Sell

As you proceed, remember that you can't sell something unless your audience believes you. The audience—people who may be for or against your argument—must feel that you are an established authority on the subject. That requires that you put some time into researching your topic.

Once you are embarked on the research, be meticulous with your outlining. With a complete outline—one that is supported by facts, statistics, quotations and/or studies—you will be armed not only with the facts but with the emotional background necessary to be convincing.

Exercise #21
The Commercial Copy

Let's see how convincing you can be as you read the commercial copy printed below. Your job in reading this copy is to get your listener's money. You are selling a product—an account at Bank of Harvard.

Remember to slate with no question, to take a moment to hear an imaginary question from a friend and to be sincere in your reply.

Say the following copy out loud. And just because this is a commercial, don't turn into a 1980s used-car salesman.

> Let's talk about your money and about where you can save it.
>
> Bank of Harvard gives you a choice of ten different savings plans.
>
> We pay the highest interest allowed by law on both passbooks and investment certificates.
>
> We give you the convenience of 1,000 offices.
>
> And, of course, online banking.
>
> If you have a question, call us, and a real person will help you 24/7.
>
> For the most complete combination of benefits you can get, save at Bank of Harvard.
>
> It's the right place for your money.

Why? This exercise is to get you in front of an audience and get a message sold. If you can sell this message, you're on the road to giving a successful persuasive speech.

Chapter Six:
Where's the Beef?

How to Persuade People to Change Their Minds

When you give a persuasive speech, it is because you believe that something needs changing. For example: *SAT's should no longer be required. Schools should be peanut-free zones. Cellphones should be automatically disabled in a car.* If you beat your audience over the head with exhortations, they will disengage and nothing will be changed. You need to show facts and cite examples, as well as mixing in something that makes your remedy easy to swallow.

Giving Your Persuasive Speech Meat

Fat makes food taste better. Unfortunately, many persuasive presentations are full of fat. Sure, fat is a key component of comfort food, but it can leave you in a food coma. You need lean meat to make people get up and fix what needs fixing.

You attempted to make your audience think like you in Exercise #18. You gave an elevator pitch in Exercise #19. You broke down the selling power of suggestion embedded in Monroe's Motivated Sequence in Exercise #20. You enhanced the power of your voice to sell a product in Exercise #21. Therefore, you know most of the elements a persuasive speech must have. You need only one more lesson: how to make sure it has meat.

What makes a persuasive speech different from an informative speech is disagreement. "The Sources of Protein" is an informative speech. "The Lies About Protein" is a persuasive speech.

I say to you, "Performance-enhancing drugs like steroids should be legalized."

"Are you kidding me? That's cheating!" you say.

"Why not? Most athletes already do it."

"Because it's wrong!"

The competing claims fly back and forth as the discussion continues. Looks like we have a disagreement here.

There must be resistance in order for there to be the need for persuasion. One force or opinion pushes against another force or opinion. For example:

> Alcohol Poses a Danger to Health
> Doctor-Assisted Suicide Is Immoral
> Everyone Should Become an Organ Donor

Some people agree with you and some people don't—that's life. And knowing how to persuade—how to present the meat of your argument—is an invaluable tool in communication.

Your purpose is to win over, not to force-feed. To make people interested in taking in what you're offering, make sure you serve up a well-prepared dish. You will need to incorporate the following elements into your speech in order to do so.

Ethos—An Ethical Appeal

This is your involvement with the moral nature of the purpose at hand. Because *you* must bring this moral aspect to the speech, you must have credibility and authority. You need to have firsthand knowledge about your topic or have done so much research that you've become an expert on it. A chubby dietician has no ethical appeal. A dental assistant with good teeth has ethical appeal.

"Athletes Need Steroid Tests Before Each Game" was the topic for a persuasive speech. One student began his speech with "I've played football for fourteen years, basketball for fifteen, and baseball for twelve. I play offensive line for Boston College. Steroid use is rampant and needs to be stopped." This speaker had a background that gave him the authority to stake out an ethical position.

Pathos—An Emotional Appeal

Your use of emotion and emotional examples will help move your audience. Stories and pictures are your best bet for accomplishing this. "My best friend was killed by a driver who was texting" is a statement that incorporates both ethos and pathos.

Logos—Logic

The proof of the validity of your argument is the meatiest part of your persuasive speech. Knocking down the opposition is the easy part. Keeping them there takes back-up. At every stage of the research process, you need to imagine your listeners saying, "Okay, but what about . . . ?" Address those "what abouts?" Prove your point with statistics, examples, pictures and quotations.

An Objective Analysis

Make sure your position is a supportable idea with a reasonable solution. A bad idea, even if sold skillfully, is still bad. "Smoking Is Good for Your Health" is not a good idea. "Football Should Be Banned" is a bad idea. Will your audience be interested in your goal? If not, you've got a tough sell.

Respect—The Golden Rule

If you are to be open-minded in listening to those who support opposing views, you have to look at the world through their eyes. This knowledge can give you the insight to help them change their focus. You wouldn't say, "I am going to present three examples that deal with why the Republican Party belongs in the nineteenth century." You want to entice your audience to listen to you, not throw spears at you. You might say instead, "I would like to discuss three issues on which the major political parties are diametrically opposed."

Focus

Keep it on your thesis statement. Sell one idea, not five.

Quality Word Choice

The twelve most persuasive words in the English language are *discovery, easy, guarantee, health, love, money, new, proven, results, safety, save* and *you*. The more you incorporate these words into your speech, the more impact you'll have on the audience.

Objectivity

I had a student who was in favor of the death penalty even though her father was in prison for murder; thirty seconds into the speech she broke down. Another student believed in doctor-assisted suicide; his mother was in the final stage of cancer, and the speech never got past the introduction. Don't attempt to present a point of view on a topic in which you are too emotionally involved.

Opinion

Never deal in it. Look at all the opinions posted on Facebook that make you crazy. I love this candidate. I hate your party. They are about as welcome as a posted picture of greasy food that some unlucky person is going to eat. And if you are speaking to an older audience, especially if you are young, your opinion means nothing if it is not backed by research.

Touch the Mind, the Heart & the Stomach

Make sure you incorporate all three into your speech: the mind, in considering the topic with objectivity; the heart, in eliciting an emotional reaction to the subject; the stomach, so that your audience will think about what the solution will mean to their wallets.

The Problem – Cause – Solution Outline

The Monroe's Motivated Sequence template is one option for constructing your persuasive speech. The Problem-Cause-Solution outline is another option.

The idea is a simple one: You set up a problem, identify a cause, and then provide a solution. Plug in your information where applicable and you're on the way to a great speech.

As an example, below I've plugged in (in regular type) the basic elements of a problem-cause-solution outline for a persuasive speech titled "Aspartame: A Chemical Monster," along with wording (in italics) the speaker used to develop the speech according to the outline.

1. Describe the problem without giving your thesis statement.

> A. Give your audience a reason to listen.
> B. Create empathy and commonality through sympathy, an awareness of jeopardy and likability—because we identify with someone we feel sorry for, worry about, or like and admire.
> C. If possible, use visuals to bring home your point.

> *One of the biggest hoaxes the public has bought into is the artificial sweetener aspartame, which is sold under several trade names, including Nutrasweet, Equal and Splenda. These sweeteners have no nutritional value and are effective as an inexpensive weight-control product. Unfortunately, the truth about aspartame doesn't stop here.*

2. Now give the thesis statement.

> A. What is the specific goal of your persuasive speech? I want to leave you with a better understanding of why it is important to ban aspartame (or donate blood, wear uniforms, vote for me).

> B. Of course, you will not say, as part of your presentation, "My thesis statement is . . ." or "I want to leave my audience with . . ." Convert your thesis into a sentence or two that shows the need for action, change or an attitude adjustment.

> Aspartame is a dangerous chemical that has many real downsides that are threats to our health. Today I will show

you three reasons why aspartame is a danger to our health and three ways to keep this poison out of your diet.

3. Lay out the cause of the problem.

    A. The main cause is . . .
    B. Another, lesser cause is . . .
    C. Another contributing cause is . . .

Aspartame is made up of three chemicals: aspartic acid, phenylalanine and methanol. Then explain how the body reacts to these chemicals and why they are dangerous.

Throughout my research I found many documents and publications pointing to the fact that many early studies done by the creators of aspartame utilized deceptive research. Then cite some of those studies and point out their flaws.

The history of how aspartame came to be approved by the FDA is riddled with manipulation and dirty politics. Explain how this was done.

4. Lay out some solutions to the problem.

    A. My first suggestion is . . .

Become educated. Here are some findings by the American Medical Association that I will pass out at the end of my speech.

    B. Second, we could . . .

Know the many foods that aspartame can be found in. Some of the products I was shocked to find it in were Alka

Seltzer, Fiber One cereal, Metamucil and children's vitamins. Show visuals of these products.

C. Third, we could . . . (this is the one you really want them to do!)

Choose other sugar substitutes like Stevia or natural sweeteners like agave or honey. Again, show visuals of products that contain these sweeteners.

5. Ask the audience to specifically decide in your favor, and be explicit about your desire for their consideration. Have you convinced your audience to look at the problem from your point of view and to agree with your solution?

I do hope after learning what the chemical compound aspartame is made of and the various side effects it is linked to—as well as the sordid, deceptive and political history it went through in order to be approved—that you will take some time to further your own investigation of it. Most important, keep you and your loved ones away from aspartame.

Depending on the circumstances, be prepared to answer questions. Some may be negative and loaded with a desire for you to react emotionally. Don't.

Having Trouble Picking a Topic?

1. Turn on the evening news and you'll find plenty of controversy. You'll also get updates on current events. Is there an election or a ballot referendum that will get your audience to pay attention?

2. What do you find yourself arguing over with your friends, your parents, your partner? Everyone feels strongly about something. Find that thing and learn how to defend it.

3. Take your favorite movie or novel and turn one of its themes into a persuasive speech. For example, "Vampires Are Real."

4. What are the majority of posts you see on Facebook, beyond the boyfriend/girlfriend drama deluge? There are plenty of forums on LinkedIn that post questions for their members to answer. Many are controversial. What's on Twitter?

5. What is a hot campus issue? This will be relevant to your audience members. One possibility: "Students with a 3.5 Average Should Not Have to Take Final Examinations."

If you're still at a loss, here's the suggested topic list I give to my students. Of course, you can take either the pro or the con position to argue:

- Boycott Walmart or any other corporation you think should be boycotted.
- Self-esteem has replaced competition in high school.
- If we do nothing, the science is clear that temperatures will continue to increase and sea levels will continue to rise.
- Cheating is out of control.
- The hybrid car is dead.
- Uniforms should be required in public schools.
- Cellphones should be disabled in restaurants and cars.
- Playstation sucks, Wii rules.
- We made the wrong choice in the 2012 presidential election.

Exercise #22
The Sheets

Come up with two possible hot topics that you will consider for a persuasive speech.

Lay out a sheet of paper for each topic. Write your stance or thesis statement on the top of each sheet. For example:

- Trampolines should be banned.
- College placement tests should not be required.
- Sugar is toxic.

Now that you have two pieces of paper with your position labeled across the top, fold the sheets in half. Write "pro" on the top of one half and "con" on the top of the other. On one half, write down and number all the pros you can cite to support your position, and on the other half write all the cons.

Some pros as well as some cons can be more extreme than others.

This list should help you decide the topic that is right for you. It will also help you look at the proposition from the opposite perspective.

Why? This is a great way to begin work on your persuasive speech and an aid that you can use any time you need to make a sound decision.

Know Your Audience

And know how to read them, especially when you are giving a persuasive speech. Audience members may vary in their ages, genders and professions, but also in their ethnicities, religious beliefs and politics. Most will be willing to listen to your point of view, but it doesn't take much to offend in a world dominated by political correctness. Your best defense is to have a warm heart and a cool head.

In a persuasive speech I gave to promote this book, I provided this quotation.

> We need great teachers, not poor ones and not mediocre ones. We have to have high standards because self-esteem comes from achievement, not from lax standards and false praise.

When I attributed the quotation to Condoleezza Rice, the former Secretary of State, you would have thought I had spit in the eye of one audience member. I certainly never meant for that citation to be an invitation to disrespectful name calling and party-bashing vitriol, but that's just what my mere mention of a name induced. I remained objective and responded by saying that I in no way meant for the gathering to turn into a political rally. My hope was that the quotation would inspire teachers and students to excellence, not mediocrity.

I walked away from that speech thankful I had never run for public office.

Always address a difficult situation the same way you approach a speech. Someone has a problem and you are offering a fix. You are the authority on the topic. Continue to believe that what you are doing is important. Be a facilitator, not an agitator. Show toughness in your persuasive speech, but never become rude.

Those in Favor

If you know your audience mostly agrees with your position on a topic but is procrastinating (I'm thinking of topics like "Take a CPR Course" or "Become an Organ Donor"), you need to get people to act. The way to do that is to provide a specific course of action around which people can rally.

What can they do? Show them in the simplest possible terms. Listeners are more likely to take action after a presentation if you can show them an easy path. Don't tell them what they should do. Show them what you did.

In a speech about the importance of organ donation, the presenter passed out cards at the end of his speech. Those who signed them and placed them next to their driver's licenses would become organ donors. That was an easy path to action.

"Books should be banned" was an audience-awakening way to open a speech titled "The Importance of Moving Beyond Recycling." The speaker then proceeded to throw his textbooks into the trash. He later got agreement from the audience that recycling is good but not creating the stuff that should be recycled is better. The presenter showed us the wonders of an e-book reader. He also showed us substitutes for plastic bottles, paper and batteries. All were easy solutions that could be and have been partially implemented.

Those Opposed

Perhaps your view is not popular among many members of your audience. A workable approach is to ask them to momentarily suspend their personal opinion and judge your position on the merits of the argument.

If your view on a topic is highly controversial—like "Universal Healthcare Is Good for Our Country" or "Capital Punishment Should Not Be Banned"—a sensible way to argue is to present points and information that lessen your listeners' negative opinions; in other words, shed more light and less heat. Remain objective and mature. It is more realistic to seek increased tolerance as opposed to a complete transformation.

The Bottom Line

In order to persuade or get your audience to simply think about your viewpoint, you must get them to listen to you. Depending on your topic, doing that may be your toughest job, so you have to lead them to an open-minded consideration of your topic.

How to do that? You must do it with tact. Set a common ground. Find something on which everyone can agree to begin with.

Exercise #23
The Persuasive Speech Intro

Your introductory statement will either grab your audience's attention or leave them looking for an exit.

Choose your topic and begin your research on your persuasive speech. This should be a topic with which you have some personal experience or with which you have a grievance. Write your thesis statement.

Think about why this topic is important to you. In your introduction, show your teacher, classmates or a family member or friend why you have passion for this topic.

Show how you have been personally affected by this topic, using a story or a picture. Then establish a smooth connection from this introduction to your thesis statement.

Why? It's time to try on the activist hat.

_____

Exercise #24
Walk in Their Shoes

Give a "con" introduction to your topic. In other words, present in your introduction a point of view that opposes yours.

If your thesis is "We should boycott Walmart," show me in a "con" introduction why "Walmart is good."

Why? What better way to know your opposition than by walking in their shoes?

What Will the Audience Remember?

I've learned from my years of teaching public speaking that people remember

>   20 percent of what they hear.
>   30 percent of what they see.
>   50 percent of what they see and hear.
>   80 percent of what they see, hear and do.

It's easy to have selective hearing. When something—like making weekend plans—screams in our ears a great deal louder than the speaker standing before us, we'll zone out. When a speaker throws in visuals, at least we have that to focus on while we're making those plans. Then there's that picture that speaks a thousand words. We zone back in. Images, which often don't need explanation, serve to enhance the point the speaker is making.

The biggest bang for the buck is to get your audience involved.

Often I will use the audience itself as a visual aid. I have everyone stand; then I ask questions about my topic that refer to them. If their answer is yes, they sit down. The first day of class I ask, *Who is taking this class because they want to learn more about how to communicate?* I'm lucky if one or two sit down. *Who is here because they hate getting up in front of an audience and want to do something about it?* More respond to this and sit. Finally, *Who is taking this class because it is a requirement?* Usually, the rest sit down. I thank them for their honesty and address all three groups' concerns and expectations.

I've known many speakers who want to make sure that 80 percent of their listeners remember their message. They have used a laptop, a soccer ball and two sections of lung to pass around: one from a healthy lung and one from a person who died of emphysema. To make sure you are making your point, get your listeners involved in hearing, seeing and doing.

"Chivalry Is Dead" may sound like a boring topic to some. A male student who was scheduled to make a presentation on that topic walked into class and gave every woman a rose. He had made his speech memorable before even giving his introduction.

The Persuasive Speech Is Where You Pull Out the Presentation Software

Persuasive speeches are ideal candidates for the use of presentation software. Graphs, numbers, group comparisons and other supporting data are best presented visually, and there are numerous tools available to help you prepare great graphics. Among the best-known are Microsoft PowerPoint, Apple KeyNote, OpenOffice Impress and such online tools as Google Documents.

No matter what your program of choice, always remember these rules:

1. Do a test run-through to make sure the equipment you are going to use shows every visual properly. Few things ruin a well-prepared presentation more decidedly than a speaker stumbling awkwardly through the controls, flipping to the wrong slide or standing in front of a blank screen. Trying to be serious with the colors of the rainbow all over your face is comical.

2. Don't put every word you're going to say on the presentation. You will find that your audience is not only just skimming the excess of words but also not listening to you fully.

3. Keep your focus on your audience, not on the visual. A momentary glance at the screen is fine, but you created the presentation and you should know what's on those slides. Your audience does not want to look at your backside for extended periods of time while you stare up at the screen.

4. Your presentation is not a display of your technical ability to produce special effects. If animations do not directly contribute to the information you are presenting, then avoid them.

5. Check the spelling and don't rely only of the spell cheek. Spelling and grammar errs will jump out at you audience and riun you're credibilty. Spell cheek wouldn't find all the errs, but your audience will, and they well focus on them instead of on what your saying. (BTW, there are 10 errors in the previous three sentences.)

6. If possible, humanize the numbers. One of the best examples of this is the 2001 iPod launch, when Steve Jobs could have said, "It holds 5GB of data." He humanized that statement by instead focusing on "1,000 songs in your pocket."

7. Practice your speech *out loud*, and do it *with* the presentation software, *before* the day of the speech.

Memorization Mayhem

I can't repeat this one enough: *Do not memorize*. Neither should you ever read a speech. So how do you strike a happy medium?

In learning a speech, the more time you put into researching, the better. During this time, you formulate ideas, gather your defense and select stories that will clarify your points, and start to store all of these in your memory.

After your research is done and your outline is complete, it's time to learn your speech. Your outline is a major aid as you commit your speech—not the exact words, but the key concepts—to your memory and prepare to deliver it to your audience.

It is easier to learn a speech in sections. Get the beginning down, then the middle, then the end. As with exercising any other skill, several repetitions daily, over a period of days, are much more effective than several hours spent on the speech in one day. Therefore, it is important to begin to learn your speech well ahead of your formal presentation.

Have confidence in your memory. Test it and keep it in good shape. Do this the same way musicians get to Carnegie Hall— practice, practice, practice.

To practice effectively, you will need a room or a car or a shower where you can be alone. You should practice there, talking out loud, with the walls for an audience. When you have said your entire speech out loud, alone, then say it to someone else. Skype is okay.

Only by speaking the words can you give them their full value. Become your own observer and hear your speech from the point of view of your audience. Then, also from their point of view, grade your speech.

Exercise #25
The
Persuasive Speech

Research it. Rehearse it. Do it—deliver it in front of the class or, if you are going this alone, Skype it. Use the Persuasive Speech Checklist for grading your speech.

Why? Because your point of view is important and can be used to enlighten others. You have a voice. Share it.

———————————————

Persuasive Speech Checklist

Now, from the point of view of an audience member, grade your speech.

1. Did the speaker use a startling statement, arouse curiosity or suspense, pose a question or tell a story in order to gain the initial attention of the audience? Yes___ No___

2. Was the purpose of the speech made clear by the thesis statement? Yes___ No___

3. Did the speaker give statistics, examples and testimony to support the thesis statement? Yes___ No___

4. Did the speaker use *ums* or *basicallys* or *you knows* or use words that his audience would have trouble understanding? Yes___ No___

5. Was the speech well organized? Yes___ No___

6. Did the speaker present a plan and show how this plan would work to bring about change? Yes___ No___

7. Did the speaker enhance a desire for change by using visuals? Yes___ No___

8. Did the speaker say exactly what we must do and how to do it in order to bring about change? Yes___ No___

9. Was the volume of the speaker's voice sufficient throughout the speech? Yes___ No___

10. Did the speaker end the speech by prompting the audience to take action or to consider his point of view? Yes___ No___

Chapter Seven:
Weapons of Mass Discussion

Career-Building Tools and Workplace Skills

Do you have any questions? A simple query like this from a less than understanding teacher led most of us into a trap at one time or another when we were in elementary or high school.

This question was a red flag for me when my American history teacher would ask it. What he was really asking was *Who of you wasn't listening?* I quickly learned not to ask questions. This is why, as a speaker, it can be tough to elicit that first question after you deliver your conclusion. Some in the audience will remember that curiosity-squelching teacher from their past.

Answering Questions Once You've Given Your Speech

If you have sparked your audience's interest, they will ask questions. If time permits, encourage your audience to ask them, saying something like *Perhaps one of my points needs further clarification.* When you put a good amount of time into the research for your speech, you will find that answering questions after your presentation is not a problem.

Make sure that when you ask *Do any points need clarification?* or say *If I can help with any questions you might have,* you never make someone feel guilty for responding to your request for questions. It's your job, as the speaker, to listen, relate and avoid drama.

Listen

There will always be someone in the audience who enjoys your presentation and someone who doesn't. One person will like your topic and point of view, and another will think it's boring or that you are a horrible person for thinking the way you do. Deal with that reality, and accept the fact that no matter what you do, you won't impress everyone.

But do note that the differing attitudes toward you and your words will affect the way your listeners will present questions. When you hear *Do you really think that?* or *In my opinion . . .*, you can be pretty sure that the questioner will seek a reaction from you.

Don't react. Simply listen to the question. Make sure you understand it before beginning your non-reactive answer. Don't let the person posing the question give a speech. Just ask him what the question is.

As a courtesy to a large group, repeat the questions as they are asked so that everyone in the audience knows what topic is being addressed.

Relate

Answer a question by drawing a comparison to the information presented in your speech. Present the facts as briefly as possible. If pressed for your opinion, give it, but support it with evidence.

If you're asked a question that can be answered with a simple yes or no, then give that simple answer. Follow up with a short clarification—supported, once again, by facts. Don't ramble or go into an explanation that is overly detailed.

If the question is *Don't you think our president is ineffective?* or *Isn't Nintendo Wii better than Playstation 3?* ask the questioner to be more specific. The president could be effective or ineffective in a wide array of situations. A game system can be compared to another one in terms of 3D mapping, tactile feedback, frame rate or availability of game titles. Don't be lured into answering such open-ended questions.

When you don't know the answer to a question, say so. But then say you'll get back to the person with the answer. Make sure you get their e-mail address or other contact information. Let them know when to expect a reply, and then stick to that date.

Avoid Drama

If someone comes at you with a question or comment that is insulting and you want to tear out either your hair or theirs, you can't. Here's where pretending comes into play again.

Remain the authority on your topic without sounding superior. Give an answer that's simple and that shows you're in control. Don't give a big smile that screams *You idiot!* at the one who has posed the question. Remain professional. Stick to the facts presented in your speech.

The Discussion: Being Persuasive in Interviews and Meetings

If you nailed your persuasive speech, you're armed with a nuke. In other words, if you know how to persuade, you know how to discuss, which is the essence of both the interview and the business meeting. In order to discuss, however, you have to shut up and let other people have their say.

The Interview: How to Be a Persuasive College Applicant or Job Seeker

The resume, your letters of recommendation and your relative with the connection may have gotten you to the door, but the prospective college or employer needs to know what they're signing up for before they let you in.

Administrators, counselors or potential bosses have seen you on paper. Now they want to see if the person behind the application or the resume matches the person speaking to them in the interview. And they would like a glimpse into your personality.

The college essay is number one and the interview is number two on the list of the things you have to ace in order to get into college. The same is true when applying for a job (substitute the resume for the essay). The interview generally makes or breaks the deal. Unfortunately, most people give the interview too little preparation time.

An interview is like going on a first date. Both are in the top ten on my list of most awkward experiences. On that first date, you have no idea if the person you are about to meet is anything like the virtual portrayal on Facebook. You hope you'll be able to keep the conversation going. You wonder whether you'll want to. You download the Bad Date Rescue app just in case the worst-case scenario materializes.

Sound familiar? But what if you pretend you've known this person for a long time? Wouldn't that lessen the awkwardness of that first face-to-face encounter?

It did for me.

So I transferred this "pretend" scenario to interviewing. I no longer thought of a job interview as a job interview. I pretended I already had the job, and thus my confidence ran ahead of my nervousness and I was comfortable with the people around me. I pretended the interview was just a meet-and-greet. I treated all the questions they asked as simple curiosity. Nor was I afraid to ask questions. By pretending, I felt I was part of the group rather than an outsider. My feeling of being at ease helped the people interviewing me see me as part of the team at their college or business.

That does not mean that I went into this meet-and-greet discussion unprepared. Here are ten considerations that will raise your comfort level and enhance the confidence and expertise you project during an interview.

1. Know what is on the piece of paper that preceded you. Any hesitations about the content of your application or resume will raise the possibility that someone else wrote it for you or that you embellished the truth.

2. Don't crack your knuckles, bite your fingernails or make fists. Displayed nervousness in your mannerisms means you'll have an adjustment period with others and not be able to just jump into your classes or work. On a luncheon interview, I spilled a glass of cola into the director's open purse. My answers must have been stellar for me to land the job after that faux pas.

3. Focus your answer and keep it succinct. Don't waste the interviewer's time while you introduce five or six thoughts and try to tie them together.

4. Eye contact, eye contact, eye contact. I have vision in only one eye. If I can make eye contact when my bad eye wanders off into never-never land, so can you.

5. Show interest. If you are not interested in what you are talking about, why should anyone else be?

6. Answer the question. *I don't know* is not an option. No *I guesses* either. A college candidate was asked, "Why do you want to go to this college?" With a shrug of his shoulders, he replied, "I don't know. I guess because my parents want me to." Do you suppose he was accepted?

7. Turn off your cell phone. Better yet, leave it in the car.

8. Do not volunteer any unacceptable work or study history to a college recruiter or potential employer. Bragging about what you got away with in high school or on your last job or saying how much you hated a high school teacher or previous boss is not a smart move.

9. Remember, no matter what they ask you, the real question is *We're about to invest in you. Are you worth it?*

10. Think about your appearance. If you plan to wear a new shirt, iron it before the interview. You don't want to look like you just popped out of a box.

Exercise #26
Off the Cuff

From the list of questions below, answer one or more. Get to the point in thirty seconds, but complete your response within one minute. Keep your answers short (though not too short), your enthusiasm high and your stories believable. In your answer, don't forget to fill in the *why*.

Grade yourself or find someone who will tell you the truth. Find out how you did on eye contact, posture, enthusiasm, the fidgeting factor, volume, word speed and grammar.

> How's your day going?
> Seen any great movies lately?
> Do you have a hobby?
> How do you handle stress?
> Tell me about you.
> What is your favorite color?
> If you could own any car, what would it be?
> Are you happy?
> Where is your favorite place to be when you have to make a tough decision?
> If you could receive a full scholarship from any college, where would it be?

Why? Speaking off the cuff is an essential part of public speaking, especially when it comes to answering questions.

The Problem with Body Language

The problem is that it speaks louder than your words—at least 90 percent louder. I saw one of my students speaking with his girlfriend outside of class one day. Her body was rigid, her face red with anger. He said, "What's wrong?" She said, "Nothing."

Your mouth says one thing while your body may clearly say another. People who see you scratching and fiddling or hear you clearing your throat countless times will be distracted from your message. What follows? They lose confidence in you. Body language, like spoken language, carries a message.

How we hold our bodies sends signals to those with whom we are communicating. When you are in a job interview and sitting before a group of interviewers, never cross your arms. Crossed arms say you are not listening. Keep an open body posture.

Lean toward the person who is asking the question, and don't forget to nod. Leaning forward is physically getting closer and says that you are interested. Leaning away or backward says that you are not interested and are trying to remove yourself from the situation.

Smile often. Ladies, before the interview, check that your teeth are lipstick free. Never smirk or shake your head. A smile communicates warmth and caring. A smirk communicates disgust and superior feelings.

We are all aware of the meaning of certain gestures. Holding your hands with the tips of your fingers touching and pointing upward is called pyramiding. It means *I am an authority*. *Thumbs up* means things are going well. *Thumbs down* means the answer is no. A *shrug of the shoulders* means I don't know or I don't care.

We all read gestures. We signal someone to sit with a wave of the hand. I have a gesture, a horizontal stroke of my hand, that signals to my family and friends "bottom line." We signal that we are listening by looking at the person who is talking and not filling in their sentences.

When we speak, gestures should accompany our spoken words. But use only your own natural gestures—the kind you use when you communicate in a friendly manner with people you are comfortable with and care about. As professional speaker and speech coach Patricia Fripp says, "Words represent your intellect. The sound, gesture and movement represent your feeling."

Remember, the same mannerisms that are ingredients for a bad speech can also keep you from doing well on a job interview. According to a 2010 CareerBuilder survey, your lack of nonverbal communicative skills can keep you from landing a job. Some nonverbals that scream *I am not right for this job* include:

> Lack of eye contact
> Lack of a smile
> Fidgeting too much
> Bad posture
> A weak handshake
> Arms crossed over your chest
> Playing with your hair or touching your face
> Using too many hand gestures

Likely Questions for Company or College Interviews

Keep in mind your purpose—to be hired or accepted. All answers should highlight why you would be a great addition to the school or organization.

1. Tell me what you know about the college/organization.

>Do your homework and be prepared with three current facts.

2. Tell me about a dilemma you had with a friend or colleague and what you did to get over it.

>Focus your answer on the resolution of the conflict. Keep the story brief. Make sure the outcome is positive.

3. What are the qualities you look for in a friend?

>*Similar interests* is a good place to start. Think about why you become friends with someone.

4. What are your greatest strengths?

>Let the interviewer see you shine as you give a brief rundown of your work-related strengths.

5. What was your favorite class in high school/college?

>Briefly describe the class, what you liked about it and how the teacher benefited you.

6. Why should I hire you/recommend you for acceptance?

Reiterate your strengths and talents that just happen to match the job description or the ideal student profile.

7. Who or what has been the most important person or event in your self-development?

Give the person's name or the description of the event. Show the interviewer how this person or event made you a stronger person.

8. When were you disappointed with a choice you made? How did you work to overcome it?

Keep the story brief. You are not in a therapist's office.

9. When I call one of your references or guidance counselors, how will they describe you?

Words like *hard-working, positive, a facilitator* and *honest* would be nice to incorporate into this answer. Be specific.

10. Finally, do you have any questions to ask me?

How long have you been at _____ and why do you like it here?

Exercise #27
Not Off the Cuff

Think about how you might answer the preceding questions.

Be specific about the university or company where you are interviewing. This will require that you check out their website. Have a parent, friend or teacher play the tough interviewer. Answer one, several or all of the ten questions.

Let the teacher, the parent or the honest friend give you feedback based on the three questions below.

On a scale of 1 to 10 (with 10 the highest), score the interviewee's answers.

- Were the interviewee's answers concise and interesting?
- Did the interviewee seem to have an agreeable and pleasing personality when answering?
- Did the interviewee's body language help or detract from her responses?

This is a great exercise for practicing your interview (meet and greet) skills. Skype, if necessary.

Why? Because the better you are at an interview, the better will be your chances of landing a rewarding job and a meaningful position.

_____

The Business Meeting

In business, discussion is simply going over the reasons for or against something. Two people or, often, a group consider an issue from opposing viewpoints. Unlike with a persuasive speech, the focus in a business discussion remains on the group or the company as a whole, not on an individual.

Any business venture requires that you collaborate. Are you tolerant of others and a good team player? Or do you become defensive at the first opportunity to get your back up?

Your goal should be to show others that you are capable of making a connection, creating comfort and building rapport. How to accomplish these three things? Through discussion.

A discussion considers a question in an open and usually informal debate. Business runs on communication, innovation and meetings. All require discussion. Here are the ground rules for planning and running a business meeting.

1. Have a specific agenda, and make sure everyone knows what the agenda is.

> a. If the meeting will be very short, state the agenda verbally.
> b. If it will last an hour or more, display a slide so the participants can keep the agenda in mind.

2. Make sure your agenda is targeted to the specific people you've invited. People in meetings generally fall into these categories:

> a. *Stakeholders* will be affected by the decisions made in the meeting. You should expect that they will participate in the discussion. If they don't, you should remind them that silence means agreement.

b. *Consumers of decisions* are not expected to be part of the decision-making process, but probably some aspect of their work will be altered by the decisions made.
c. *Passive listeners* just need to know what's going on.

3. When questions and discussion arise in the meeting:

a. Make sure you understand the question. If there is the slightest doubt, before you answer, ask for clarification, or rephrase the question in your own terms and ask if that is what was meant.
b. Make sure the person talking understands your response (though it may not be the response they wanted).

4. If the discussion veers off the agenda, do one of the following:

a. When it's a short segue that might add information to the current topic, try to fit it in.
b. When it's heading toward other topics but still useful, make a specific note, and make sure everyone interested knows you'll continue discussing this in another meeting.
c. When it appears useless, ask why it relates to the topic. The result will be, on a good day, either a good explanation, or a *Never mind, we can talk about it later*.

5. Make clear the point at which the meeting has covered the agenda and is ended.

a. When you have covered your agenda items and there are no more questions, close the meeting. Don't let it drift onto other topics. If other topics need attention, schedule another meeting.

b. End the meeting on time. Chances are the attendees have other appointments and can't hang around while your meeting runs beyond its stated schedule.

6. Publish the results of the meeting. You are the meeting leader; only you can identify the important information that attendees should have heard.

a. Were the agenda items all covered?
b. What decisions were made?
c. What issues or concerns need further discussion, and who is responsible for following up?
d. Did other issues arise that warrant other meetings on different topics?

Exercise #28
Rock the Boat

Choose one of the following topics and discuss it with a group, following the guidelines presented in the section "The Business Meeting," above.

- Financial planning will take the place of math in senior year.
- There will be a mandatory parent meeting to inform parents about new drug-testing rules.
- Morality will be a required course in high school.
- The use of taurine in energy drinks should be banned.
- The ACT and SAT will no longer be deciding factors for college acceptance.
- Texting will be banned in restaurants.
- Those with a 3.5 average or higher do not need to take final examinations.

After your discussion, present a report (in hard-copy form) of your findings to the principal, division chair or teacher or a friend who has agreed to be an objective observer.

Why? To put your public-speaking skills into action in a decision-making environment.

Chapter Eight:
Red Bull for the Soul

Providing Direction for Yourself and Your Audience by Motivating

As you prepare for your final speech presentation, I'd like you to recall that the potential for a great speech exists when the speaker has a passion for the topic, the knowledge to explain that topic clearly, and the ability to leave an audience wanting more.

Do you remember Exercise #1: The Nightmare? You were asked to turn off your mobile device, to power down. Then you were asked to remember and say four things: your name, where you were born, where you live now and where you see yourself in five years. All are important, but the last question was the first step to the last exercise in this book. For many, this last exercise becomes a life changer.

By now, you have probably flipped or scrolled to the back of the book to check out Exercise #33: The Road You Took. I can imagine that some of you are saying, *You want me to do what?!*

Hear me out.

When we begin a trip to an unfamiliar location, most of us use TomTom or Google Maps to plan our course. In contrast, when it comes to our life's destinations, we rarely have a "to" location or an interactive map to lead us there.

A recent study at Dominican University, conducted by Dr. Gail Matthews, shows the effectiveness of knowing where you are going and writing down that destination. The participants in the study who wrote down their goals, shared them with a friend, and sent updates on their progress were 33 percent more successful in accomplishing their stated goals than those who didn't.

What do you want to accomplish in the next ten years? What would you like to do professionally? Envision this dream. Take that mental leap—be it wild or practical. Maybe you're not sure. That's fine.

Changing your mind is okay, but you do need a goal for the next exercise. It will not only become the basis for your next speech, but possibly a blueprint for your life.

Exercise #29
Improve Your Odds

Fill in the blank below, and not just mentally. Write it down.

Ten years from now I want to be

_____.

Clarity is power.

Now you need to figure out the steps necessary to get where you want to be. Make a conscious effort to understand the steps you will have to take in order to see your goals realized.

With that blank filled in, consider the answers to the following questions, then write down your answers from a point of view ten years in your future.

1. Why did you want this dream? (The answer can date back to your childhood or be something more recent.)

2. What education did you pursue? (What have others done to get where you want to go? Luck is not an option. Schools, universities, internships are.)

3. Who or what inspired you along the way? (Many students who have chosen to enter the military say their decision was a direct result of 9/11.)

4. What part of your career history led to your success? (The job or degree that led to the next job or degree that led to . . .)

5. What obstacles did you overcome? (Physical, mental, emotional—all could play into this one.)

6. Are you content with where you are now? (Remember, you're answering as if you're ten years older than you are now.)

Why? Preparation equips us to fulfill a dream. Many dreams fail because people are not properly prepared for what they attempt to do. Know your dream and then seek the route to that destination.

The Motivational Speech

All the speeches you give should contain elements of motivation. In the demonstration speech, you motivate your audience to try what you just showed them how to do. In the informative speech, you motivate your audience to seek more information about your topic. In the persuasive speech, you motivate your audience to agree with your position on a topic. In the motivational speech, you motivate your audience to be more and do more.

What is the thought or feeling that gets you going? What gets me exercising every day is that I know I look better when I exercise regularly. Exercise is not always comfortable, and at times it's even painful. But when I look better, I feel better, and then I do better. That's my motive, my incentive, my reason for staying focused on a daily workout. What's yours?

The motivational speech comes in many forms—the inspirational speech, the sermon, the commemorative talk, the eulogy, the graduation speech. The unifying theme in all of these and other motivational speeches is that they unlock potential and challenge us to never give up our dreams. They encourage us to strive for excellence.

These speeches praise and celebrate life's achievements by drawing from examples, testimony, even statistics. These speeches leave the audience with respect for the person or group described.

Motivational speeches are the Red Bull that gives us a kick and keeps us moving forward when it would be so much easier to stop. Change happens when we do what we don't want to do or are afraid to do.

The Red Bull found in the power of words helps us do those things. It leaves the audience with the sense that they could achieve greatness—be it in an extraordinary setting or in one that's ever so humble.

Attend a Weight Watchers meeting and you will hear a motivational speech. Listen to a good sermon and you will be empowered through inspiration. Watch any sports movie and the coach will lead the team to victory with his motivational speech. Do Al Pacino in *Any Given Sunday* and Denzel Washington in *Remember the Titans* ring a bell? If not, YouTube, watch and listen. If you're a Lord of the Rings fan, remember King Theoden's speech before his troops ride into battle in defense of Minas Tirith?

What the Motivational Speech Must Have

Your motivational speech is the culmination of your work for this book. It will be as big as your dreams, because it is about your dreams. Make sure you've got all the following bases covered.

The ability to relate. Don't tell me what it's like to lose weight if you haven't successfully fought the battle yourself. If you went to a $5,000-a-week health spa in the Berkshires and stayed there for a month to lose weight, that's nice, but I need to know what happens in the real world.

A roadmap. How did you get there, and how can I follow, step by step? *It takes a lot of hard work* is not a roadmap.

Compassion but not pity. Good speakers understand the trials we all must face, but they never treat themselves or their audience as victims.

Motivational quotations. What someone else says is okay, but the quotations that come from your heart are the best. These words came from a single mother who went from addict to bartender to nurse: *The best way to like yourself is to do something you are proud of.*

Words I will remember, stories I can relate to and accomplishments that are attainable. Bring home to your audience how your experiences have either made you stumble or moved you forward.

No apples thrown at the audience. You never see an apple tree throwing apples. A tree doesn't shout, *I've got the best apples*, and then hit you in the face. If an apple tree looks like it has ripe apples and I'm hungry for apples, I will choose that tree and pick my apples there. In other words, don't boast.

A character arc. Where'd you start out? What happened to make you change? What did you do to make things better? How did you change? *I didn't even know what business was when I decided to major in it at B.U.* That one sentence speaks reams. We don't need every little detail—just a few sentences about your life thus far.

Believability. Does your story sound too good to be true? Show me that it's not. And show me that I can do it too.

You are going to give your audience a life lesson, and speeches like this are not started just by walking to a podium and beginning to talk. This speech requires a formal introduction.

Introducing a Speaker

When you deliver a speech in front of a class or a few friends, it is not likely that someone will introduce you. That's your job, and we covered that back in Chapter One.

But at a formal occasion—an assembly, a graduation, a media event—someone will introduce the guest speaker. If that someone is you, you should follow these guidelines and remember that no one came to this event to hear an introduction, so anything you have to say should be brief.

1. Acknowledge the event. If this is a special occasion, make sure your initial comment refers to it, as these opening statements do.

- "Congratulations to the class of 2022 . . ."
- "Today marks the anniversary of 9/11, and we are honored to have with us . . ."
- "I have a story about our next speaker that I think the Glee Club will find entertaining."

2. Tell me why you are interested in this speaker. Is this person a friend? Is she a mentor? Along your path to wisdom, has this person affected you?

- "I first met our guest speaker when we were both in Professor Warren's speech class . . ."
- "*Happiness comes from striving, doing, loving, achieving, conquering. Always something positive.* These words have shaped my life. These words were once spoken to me by

my mentor and a man I am proud to say is our guest speaker."

3. Tell me three pertinent, current and interesting things about the speaker.

- Our guest speaker is a graduate of Mount Wachusett Community College.
- She went on to receive her Master of Political Science degree from Harvard University.
- And with your vote, Algonquin Niebergall will soon be Governor Algonquin Niebergall.

4. Introduce your speaker. Let the name flow off of your lips without looking down at a note card. Make sure your pronunciation is correct. Start the applause and let the speaker begin the walk to the podium.

- I am honored to introduce to you my mentor and the next governor of Massachusetts, Algonquin Niebergall.

5. Shake the hand of the person you introduced as he or she approaches the podium and the audience applauds.

Exercise #30
The Formal Introduction of That Special Person

Back in the beginning of *Show, Don't Tell*, you learned to express how proud you are of your name when introducing yourself to an audience. I suggested that you pretend to be introducing yourself to someone you really wanted to meet.

For me this person is Liza Minnelli. Who is that person for you?

Pretend that person is the keynote speaker at your graduation from high school or college. You are one of the graduates, and you have been asked to introduce this speaker.

Why? Because the quality of your introduction sets the stage for the speaker. Will the audience want to hear more after your introduction?

_____

Exercise #31
The Formal Introduction of You

Make sure you have completed Exercise #29: Improve Your Odds before taking on this exercise.

Team up with a classmate or friend and have him or her introduce you, following the guidelines presented in the section "Introducing a Speaker," above. This is another graduation ceremony, but ten years from now, and this time you are the keynote speaker.

You will have to tell your classmate how you filled in the big blank in Exercise #29. The story of what you have done in those ten years will be part of your classmate's introduction of you.

Then, reverse roles.

If you are solo, how would you introduce yourself at the formal graduation ceremony?

Why? Again, the quality of this introduction sets the stage for the speaker. Will the audience want to hear more from the keynote speaker after this introduction?

———————————————————

Your Motivational Speech

In order to give this speech as if you are looking back over the past ten years, you should have in mind that plan or path you embarked on after you filled in that blank.

Ten years from now I want to be

_____.

Remember, this is not what a parent or a partner thinks you should be when you grow up. What do *you* want?

Delve deeper.

If you want to be an actor, be specific. Your own sitcom? A starring role in a movie? The lead in a Broadway show? *Famous* is not specific.

If you want to be successful in business, be specific. Your own business? Your title? Your product? Your dot-com? *Rich* is not specific.

If you want to be a doctor, be specific. Your specialty? Your hospital? *Kinda like one of those doctors on television* is not specific.

You can get what you want when you are willing to take the necessary actions to support your intention. Go over in detail the steps that will move you forward to your goal.

If you have plotted your route and taken the imaginary journey, you have the backbone of your speech, but only the backbone. Remember, this is a motivational speech, not a verbal rendering of your resume, a pity party or a self-fest.

One of the worst motivational speeches I've heard was given by a speaker who talked about himself for fifteen minutes and then said, "But forget about me." What!? Then he spent thirty seconds dishing out hackneyed expressions like *follow your dreams, never give up, last but not least, every coin has two sides, go-team-go.* By the end I wanted to scream. In other words, he did nothing but throw apples and spout clichés.

One of the best motivational speeches I've heard was given by a soldier who served in Afghanistan. When he returned home, his life had no direction. He began his speech by giving a one-minute synopsis of his two tours of duty. He then said, "You are the heroes seated before me." He went on to explain that the real hero gets up every day and fights for his dream and achieves it. His projection ten years into the future was that he would be the owner of a solar energy company. At the end of the speech he asked, "What will be the trademark of your character?"

Another great speech was given by a future special needs teacher who began her speech with "I don't need to tell you that you've got a lot of problems." She ended her speech with "Don't be pushed by your problems; be led by your dreams." During her presentation she showed us how this philosophy had worked for her and helped her become the Teacher of the Year.

Before you go off on any story, make sure it relates to your thesis statement. What do you want to leave your audience with a better understanding of? You have a story, but get to the point.

Keep to an Outline and Frame Your Motivational Speech with Interesting Rhetoric

What's rhetoric? Words or phrases positioned in an interesting and memorable way. Martin Luther King's "I Have a Dream" speech is a stellar example. Using metaphor, experience, and repetition he created an effective, even iconic speech about racism.

Another great example was from a student who began his speech with a rhetorical question: *Who do you want to make proud of you? Think about it.* He repeatedly posed this question as he took us briefly through his high school experience, his college experience, his experience at a college he transferred to and his experience in grad school on through to his current success as a father and a chief financial officer.

Another example was a speech in which we were led along the path to success of a speaker whose thesis statement was *The moment you stop taking chances is the moment you stop getting them.* She told us how that philosophy had led her at first to disaster, but finally to success. She introduced each section of her speech by repeating her thesis statement.

"No" inched me closer to "yes" is another favorite. Rejection stinks, but it can also change your life for the better. This speaker, who had reached her goal, went on to explain. She told about getting a "no" from all her top college choices and how this led her to take a gap year to reevaluate her priorities. Then she described the "no" from MTV that led her to NBC and the "no" from her doctor that led her to return to the country where she had spent that gap year so she could adopt her first baby.

This Is Your Life, But So What!

If your imagined life—what has happened from where you are now to where you will be in ten years—were filmed as a movie, what is this movie about? Every movie, whether it's an action thriller or a monster movie or an irreverent comedy, is about something. That something is either an answer to a question or a debate about the pros and cons of a particular point of view. What's yours?

The theme in *Saving Private Ryan* is "One man counts." The theme is framed as a movie about World War II, but it's really the importance of one man.

The theme in *Legally Blonde* is "It's a problem being looked down upon for being pretty and blonde, and what to do about it."

The theme in *The King's Speech* is "You have a voice, and no matter what it takes, you need to find it."

Tell me about *your* journey, but show me how to reach *my* destination.

A motivational speech I heard used the poem "The Road Not Taken" by Robert Frost as a framework. The poem related to the theme of the speech, for the speaker's life had taken him on an unexpected road. He recited one of the verses and explained what it meant in his life.

Read this poem and let it serve as an inspiration. Think about your dream, and possibly even re-think your dream. Ten years from now, are you doing what you want to do, or what someone else wants you to do?

Exercise #32
The Road Not Taken

Recite this poem, concentrating on the meaning. Bring into focus
the picture the poet has drawn with words.

The Road Not Taken

Two roads diverged in a yellow wood,
And sorry I could not travel both
And be one traveler, long I stood
And looked down one as far as I could
To where it bent in the undergrowth;

Then took the other, as just as fair,
And having perhaps the better claim
Because it was grassy and wanted wear;
Though as for that, the passing there
Had worn them really about the same,

And both that morning equally lay
In leaves no step had trodden black.
Oh, I kept the first for another day!
Yet knowing how way leads on to way,
I doubted if I should ever come back.

I shall be telling this with a sigh
Somewhere ages and ages hence;
Two roads diverged in a wood, and I—
I took the one less traveled by,
And that has made all the difference.

Speak the verses aloud to experience the thoughts and feelings
the poet communicates. Let them also inspire you to think about
your dream.

Speak slowly so that your audience has time to see the image you paint with Frost's words. By the end of the poem, make apparent—through your tone—whether you made the right decision. Only through the way you speak the poet's words will the audience know.

Why? To bring color and meaning to words through your interpretation and voice.

Alert – Alert – Alert

You are contemplating your future and researching how to get there. Kudos, if you have begun to outline your motivational speech. Now don't blow it by writing down the speech word for word.

If you absolutely must write out your speech, go ahead. But then turn it into an outline, and once you've completed the outline, throw away the written-out version. Otherwise, the temptation to read your speech will be stronger than that exerted by a hot-fudge sundae with triple fudge oozing down a pile of homemade vanilla-bean ice cream.

Let's go through the outline template we worked with in Chapter Three and plug your motivational speech into that.

Recall that the first two questions of the template (title and purpose) are not part of the presentation of your speech; they are just part of the preparation to help clarify your thoughts.

What is the title of my speech? Just as with a movie title, the title of your speech is a series of words that sums it up: "The Road

Taken," "Life's a Bitch," "Rebel With a Cause." From the title, the message of the speech follows naturally.

What is the purpose of my speech? In other words, I want to leave my audience with a better understanding of

_____.

> What the road to success looks like, or
> How difficult it is to really succeed in business without really trying, or
> How I was out of my league and became a player in the majors, or
> The meaning of life.

Now you fill in the blank.

How will I open the speech to get my audience's attention? This is where the speech presentation begins. Know the audience you will address. Begin with an acknowledgment of the event. *Congratulations, Class of 2022!* or *Thank you for asking me to be a part of your Weight Watchers meeting this evening.* Or open by establishing a common bond with your audience: *I too once sat in this auditorium waiting for my diploma and hoping the keynote speaker would get it over with.* Then tell a story, read a quotation, cite a statistic or ask a question that will lead into your theme.

What is my statement of purpose? Reveal to the audience in a simple sentence the theme of your motivational speech. During Oprah Winfrey's last show, she revealed her theme perfectly. She said that in her show's run of twenty-five years, she never missed one day: "This is what I was called to do. . . . Everybody has a calling, and your real job in life is to figure out what that is and to get about the business of doing it.

What main points do I want to make that will keep "I'm interested" written all over those faces? You need to support your theme! Here's where you tell the audience about your journey and show them how to walk on water. What was your experience, and what is your advice that will give them the motivation to strive for the best?

What examples, anecdotes, humor, statistics, quotations or other information can I use to support my main points? Make sure each one supports your theme.

How can I entertain the audience? Use the power of your voice to punctuate your words of experience and wisdom.

How can I summarize briefly what I have said to make my audience remember my main points? In conclusion . . . To wrap up . . . What I would most like you to remember about this time together is . . . Take any of these three suggestions and complete the sentence. Review your main points and tie them to the theme. A student who projected herself as a successful writer ten years in the future spoke about conquering fear. She said, "I look at all of you and know you've all had troubles, but you're all here. You haven't let those imperfections of life stop you. Those imperfections should inspire us to work, to overcome, to love life."

How will I close my speech? This is just the punctuation mark at the end of the summary. Do you have a final quotation you can use to end the speech? Another story? My favorite is to refer back to my opening story, quotation or statistic. The future novelist closed with, "If we can find beauty in the dirt and joy in the tears, the motivation to create and continue through struggles and tragedies, then we may consider ourselves truly free. Thank you and blessings to the class of 2022."

Exercise #33
The Road You Took

Now it is your turn. It is ten years in the future. You have been asked to be the keynote speaker at your former high school or college graduation ceremony. You have been asked because you have achieved great success in your chosen field.

Yes, this requires a major dose of thought, imagination, research and planning. With your words and your experiences, inspire your audience to achieve their dreams too.

This speech is not a recitation of your resume. It is a call for others to succeed—with you as the example.

Give your motivational presentation to the class. Make it ten to fifteen minutes in length. If you have the choice of speaking in a larger facility than a classroom, do that. The bigger the room, the better. This is your last speech of this book, so make a production out of it.

Why? To show us how we too can have a dream fulfilled.

Motivational Speech Checklist

Did you follow the guidelines for the section "What the Motivational Speech Must Have," earlier in this chapter? Did you leave your audience wanting more?

Remember how you sounded in Exercise #1? If you did all the exercises in this book and did them with purpose, you owe yourself and everyone else in the class a standing ovation. You have definitely developed confidence just by stepping out of your comfort zone and into accomplishment. When you speak well, you feel strong. Use that strength to strengthen others.

Now you're speaking like a pro!

Bravo!

Appendix A: Irregular Verbs

Present	Past	PastPerfect
awake	awoke	awoken
bear	bore	borne
beat	beat	beat
become	became	become
begin	began	begun
bend	bent	bent
beset	beset	beset
bet	bet	bet
bid	bid/bade	bid/bidden
bind	bound	bound
bite	bit	bitten
bleed	bled	bled
blow	blew	blown
break	broke	broken
breed	bred	bred
bring	brought	brought
broadcast	broadcast	broadcast
build	built	built
burn	burned/burnt	burned/burnt
burst	burst	burst
buy	bought	bought
cast	cast	cast
catch	caught	caught
choose	chose	chosen
cling	clung	clung
come	came	come
cost	cost	cost
creep	crept	crept

cut	cut	cut
deal	dealt	dealt
dig	dug	dug
dive	dived/dove	dived
do	did	done
draw	drew	drawn
dream	dreamed/dreamt	dreamed/dreamt
drive	drove	driven
drink	drank	drunk
eat	ate	eaten
fall	fell	fallen
feed	fed	fed
feel	felt	felt
fight	fought	fought
find	found	found
fit	fit	fit
flee	fled	fled
fling	flung	flung
fly	flew	flown
forbid	forbade	forbidden
forget	forgot	forgotten
forego/forgo	forewent	foregone
forgive	forgave	forgiven
forsake	forsook	forsaken
freeze	froze	frozen
get	got	gotten
give	gave	given
go	went	gone
grind	ground	ground
grow	grew	grown
hang	hung	hung
hear	heard	heard
hide	hid	hidden
hit	hit	hit

hold	held	held
hurt	hurt	hurt
keep	kept	kept
kneel	knelt	knelt
knit	knit	knit
know	knew	know
lay	laid	laid
lead	led	led
leap	leaped/leapt	leaped/leapt
learn	learned	learned
leave	left	left
lend	lent	lent
let	let	let
lie	lay	lain
light	lighted/lit	lighted
lose	lost	lost
make	made	made
mean	meant	meant
meet	met	met
misspell	misspelled	misspelled
mistake	mistook	mistaken
mow	mowed	mowed/mown
overcome	overcame	overcome
overdo	overdid	overdone
overtake	overtook	overtaken
overthrow	overthrew	overthrown
pay	paid	paid
plead	pled	pled
prove	proved	proved/proven
put	put	put
quit	quit	quit
read	read	read
rid	rid	rid
ride	rode	ridden
ring	rang	rung

rise	rose	risen
run	ran	run
saw	sawed	sawed/sawn
say	said	said
see	saw	seen
seek	sought	sought
sell	sold	sold
send	sent	sent
set	set	set
sew	sewed	sewed/sewn
shake	shook	shaken
shave	shaved	shaved/shaven
shear	shore	shorn
shed	shed	shed
shine	shone	shone
shoe	shoed	shoed/shod
shoot	shot	shot
show	showed	showed/shown
shrink	shrank	shrunk
shut	shut	shut
sing	sang	sung
sink	sank	sunk
sit	sat	sat
sleep	slept	slept
slay	slew	slain
slide	slid	slid
sling	slung	slung
slit	slit	slit
smite	smote	smitten
sow	sowed	sowed/sown
speak	spoke	spoken
speed	sped	sped
spend	spent	spent
spill	spilled	spilled

spin	spun	spun
spit	spit/spat	spit
split	split	split
spread	spread	spread
spring	sprang/sprung	sprung
stand	stood	stood
steal	stole	stolen
stick	stuck	stuck
sting	stung	stung
stink	stank	stunk
stride	strode	stridden
strike	struck	struck
string	strung	strung
strive	strove	striven
swear	swore	sworn
sweep	swept	swept
swell	swelled	swelled/swollen
swim	swam	swum
swing	swung	swung
take	took	taken
teach	taught	taught
tear	tore	torn
tell	told	told
think	thought	thought
thrive	thrived/throve	thrived
throw	threw	thrown
thrust	thrust	thrust
tread	trod	trodden
understand	understood	understood
uphold	upheld	upheld
upset	upset	upset
wake	woke	woken
wear	wore	worn
weave	weaved/wove	weaved/woven
wed	wed	wed

weep	wept	wept
wind	wound	wound
win	won	won
withhold	withheld	withheld
withstand	withstood	withstood
wring	wrung	wrung
write	wrote	written

Appendix B: Nuked Charades

Red Things
Devil
Fire
Heart
Hair
Nail polish
Lipstick
Flag
Carpet
Dress
Eyes

Things In Cars
Steering wheel
Horn
Mirror
Seats
Cup holder
Wheels
Radio
Wipers
Brakes
Transmission

Things Feet Do
Walk
Tap
Kick
Run
Slip
Ache
Skip
Jump
Slide
Dance

Things Actors Do
Auditions
Sign autographs
Puts on makeup
Flops
Gets nervous
Forgets lines
Cries
Stars
Rehearses
Gets fired

Weapons

Hand grenade
Rifle
Slingshot
Pea shooter
Tear gas
Knife
Pistol
Fist
Bomb
Poison

Things To Wash

Babies
Hair
Hands
Dishes
Clothes
Fingernails
Floor
Silverware
Dogs
Eyeglasses

House Chores

Vacuum
Mop
Paint
Wash clothes
Cook
Iron
Clean windows
Fold clothes
Empty garbage
Make bed

Sharp Things

Knife
Pin
Axe
Needle
Razor
Glass
Student
Teeth
Nails
Claws

Things That Are Heavy

Suitcase
Barbells
Heart
Legs
Child
Television
Bed
Chair
Car
Horse

Things in a Hardware Store

Rake
Paint brush
Hammer
Nails
Rope
Tape measure
Screw driver
Hedge clippers
Lawn mower
Shovel

Things in School
Books
Teacher
Lap tops
Exams
Cheating
Cheerleaders
Clock watcher
Drama
Chairs
Black or white board

Things Found in a Clothing Store
Suit
Dress
Jeans
Raincoat
Vest
Tie
Belt
Jewelry
Sweaters
Gloves

Electronic Devices
Cell phone
Television
Stereo
Game boy
Ipod
Camera
Calculator
Ipad
Lap top
GPS

Things a Wife Does That Aggravate Her Husband
Snores
Nags
Buys
Cries
Gains weight
Gets drunk
Forgets
Gossips
Yells
Chews her nails

Sources Consulted

Barton, Robert. *Acting Onstage and Off*. Belmont, CA: Wadsworth/Thomson Learning, 2003.

Brooke, Tucker, ed. *Shakespeare's Principal Plays*. New York: D. Appleton-Century Company, 1935.

"Business Tips from the Sharks." ABC Shark Tank. ABC, 2012. 13 Sept. 2012. http://abc.go.com/shows/shark-tank/tips/ThemeGallery/777022.

Chmielewiski, Gary. *The Classroom Zone: Jokes, Riddles, Tongue Twisters and "Daffinitions."* Chicago: Norwood House Press, 2008.

Emrich, Duncan, ed. *The Nonsense Book of Riddles, Rhymes, Tongue Twisters, Puzzles and Jokes from American Folklore*, 3rd ed. New York: Four Winds Press, 1971.

"Etiquette: Protocol of Introducing People," 3 Nov. 2007. www.rightattitudes.com/2007/.../etiquette-protocol-introducing-peopl...

Frost, Robert. *Collected Poems of Robert Frost*. New York: Halcyon House, 1940.

Hastings, S. E. *Miss Mary Mac All Dressed in Black: Tongue Twisters, Jump-Rope Rhymes and Other Children's Lore from New England*. Little Rock, AR: August House, 1990.

Matthews, Gail. "Study Backs Up Strategies for Achieving Goals." Newsroom, Dominican University of California, n.d. 4 Sept. 2012.

http://www.dominican.edu/dominicannews/study-backs-up-strategies-for-achieving-goals.

McMillan, Don. "How Not to Use a Powerpoint." 2009. YouTube. 13 Sept. 2012. http://www.youtube.com/watch?v=GB7S-KOJIfE&playnext=1&list=PL84E229F0B4A5C911

Opie, Iona, and Peter Opie, eds., *The Oxford Dictionary of Nursery Rhymes.* Oxford, England: Oxford University Press, 1951.

 "Some Men See Things as They Are and Ask Why I Dream Things That Never Were and Ask Why Not. What Did Robert F. Kennedy Mean When He Said That?" Wiki Answers. Jan. 2011. http://wiki.answers.com/Q/Some_men_see_things_as_they_are_and_ask_why_I_dream_things_that_never_were_and_ask_why_not_What_did_Robert.F.Kennedy_mean_when_he_said_that

Swain, John Howard. *The Science and Art of Commercial Acting.* John Howard Swain. 2008.

Sykes, Charles J. *Fifty Rules Kids Won't Learn in School.* New York: St. Martin's Press, 2007.

Walters, Lily. *Secrets of Successful Speakers.* New York: McGraw-Hill, 1993.

www.ingramcontent.com/pod-product-compliance
Lightning Source LLC
LaVergne TN
LVHW051519080426
835509LV00017B/2116